WITHDRAWN

Jere Hochman

Thinking About Middle School

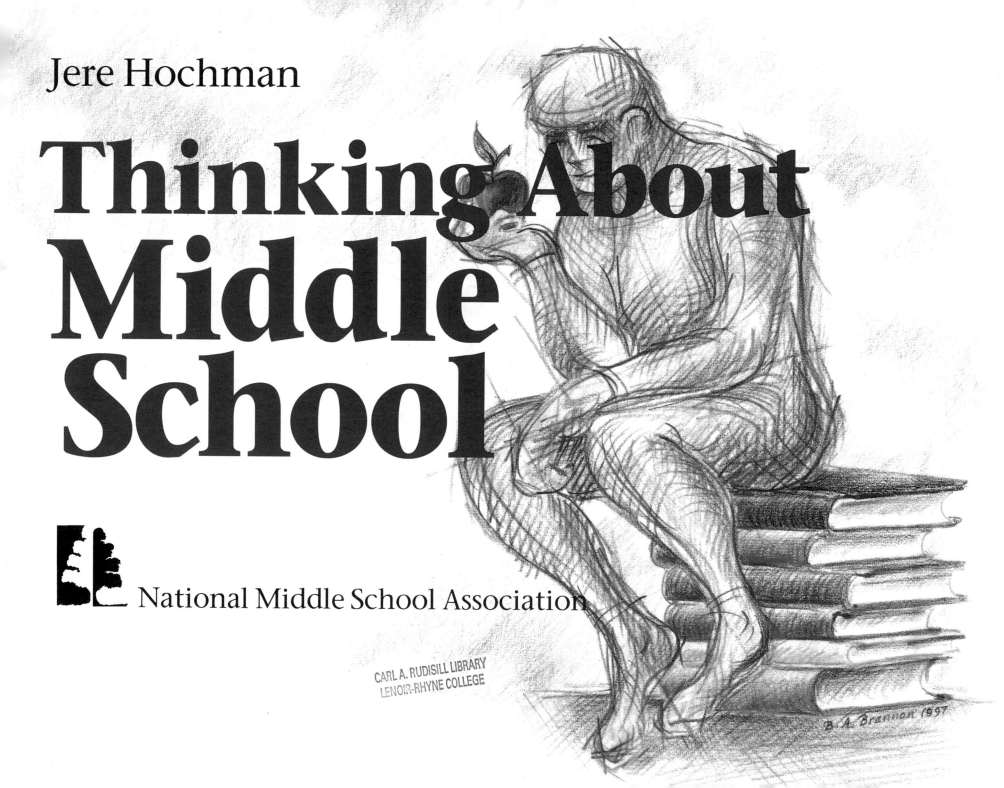

B.A. Brennon 1997

National Middle School Association
2600 Corporate Exchange Drive, Suite 370
Columbus, Ohio 43231
Telephone (800) 528-NMSA

Sue Swaim, Executive Director
Jeff Ward, Director of Business Services
John Lounsbury, Editor
Mary Mitchell, Copy Editor/Designer
Marcia Meade, Publications Sales

ISBN: 1-56090-122-5   NMSA Stock Number: 1249

...to Josette

and

Benjamin and Emily Jane

About the Author

Dr. Jere Hochman began teaching eighth graders unified studies (interdisciplinary English and social studies) in 1974 and served as a middle school principal in two districts between 1984 and 1993. He is currently Superintendent of the Parkway School District in St. Louis, Missouri. Jere received his doctorate from Teachers College, Columbia University after acquiring earlier degrees at the University of Missouri-St. Louis.

Married and the father of two children, Jere runs marathons and reads anything related to the brain and learning.

Contents

Preface

This is NOT a book about *teaming, advisory, interdisciplinary units, intramurals, parent-teacher conferences,* and other middle school issues.

Rather, it's a book about *THINKING ABOUT* teaming, advisory, interdisciplinary units, intramurals, parent-teacher conferences, and other middle school issues.

This book will not dangle phrases in front of you like "93% of all award winning middle schools have advisory programs" or "middle school youngsters require structure, clear expectations, and limits."

Rather, this book will challenge you to think about phrases like "the problem with whole language is that most teachers just switched to teaching the other half" or "they didn't have to teach algebra at Woodstock."

This is not a HOW TO book about middle school.
   It's a WHY? book about middle school.

This is not a WHAT? book about middle school.
   It's a SO WHAT? book about middle school.

The meaning that matters in this book is not the author's.
   The meaning that matters in this book is yours.

Enjoy!

CHAPTER 1 Thinking about...

Your first thoughts about middle school:
(use the space below)

Really, I'm serious. Go ahead — *use the space below.*

TIME OUT: Choose your own adventure...or how to read this book!

If your world is **left-brained**, linear, and concrete-sequential:

1) first, number the items on the next page and add an item "#9. All of the above"— and bubble it in.

2) Second, get out your yellow highlighter, and then,

3) third, proceed to think about middle school.

If your world is **right-brained**, networked, and abstract (you probably won't read the pages in order anyway, but just in case), consider the items that follow as the stuff of your portfolio, the windows on your monitor, the bubbles in your mind map, or the clippings for your collage. Then get out your pens; prepare to draw circles, arrows, and marginal notes (we've left you a lot of room in the margins to react); and start thinking about middle school.

If your map is one which criss-crosses the city and you find yourself drawing "the big picture" on the chalkboard every chance you get (personally, I can't think without a pen in hand or a flip chart at my right), prepare yourself. You are in for a cognitive treat.

If your road is the information highway, write me at JHSTL@aol.com.

If your life's highway is to and from school:

1. (to) skip everything up to page 8, "Time Out" and follow the Roman numerals for the outline of this book and

2. (from) begin comparing your world to the sections that seem most relevant to you and read them.

And, if you are one of those folks who asks before a faculty meeting "do we need to bring a pencil" or shows up at a workshop without something to scribble notes with, then either:

1. your school spends way too much time on business, or

2. you think no one has anything s/he can teach you — but either way, you probably aren't interested in learning anything new; so do yourself a favor and give this book to someone else. If you proceed you'll just get frustrated or defensive.

Thinking about middle school?

:-)   Does he mean there should be thinking all around the middle school? Is he inferring that there isn't thinking going on in classrooms? Is he referring to kids? teachers? administrators? (Administrators thinking always gets a chuckle).

:-/   Does he mean we should think about the topic of middle school?

:-| Is this about thinking as in critical thinking or just regular thinking?

:-(Should we be thinking about our middle school? We are in a junior high.

:->   Or, is this a book that will help us think about middle school? or about thinking about thinking in the middle school? or about thinking about how to think about middle school?

:=)   Reflective practice! That's it. If we just took a little time (if we had the time) to think about school, teaching, what works, what might work ... or should we ...?

:-}   Sure, but should we think about the day to day, the nuts and bolts, the what makes it tick ... or the concept, the theory, you know, when we say "that's against middle school philosophy" whenever we see a change we don't like?

:=)   I've got it. Thinking about how I think about ...

YES!
YES!
YES!
YES!
YES!
YES!
YES!
and
YES!

...   thinking all around the middle school

...   think about the topic of middle school

...   critical thinking and just regular thinking

...   thinking about our middle school ... junior high

...   think about middle school ... think about thinking in the middle school

...   reflective practice

...   think about the day to day, the nuts and bolts, the what makes it tick ... and the concept, the theory, and

...   thinking about how you think (about) (that's right—how do YOU think? how do YOU think about schooling? DO YOU think about schooling?

about

around

above

to

in

through

with

Thinking (preposition) **Middle School**

near

under

behind

beyond

for

before

toward

The second step in thinking about middle school, no matter what your preferred method of "thinking about," is to consider how you define SUCCESSFUL SCHOOLING.

This isn't the "vision thing" nor is it the mission statement.

This is success, plain and simple. How do we know we're doing what we should be doing, and doing it well?

And in the middle school, and in school in general, it's quite easily defined without all the technical, quantitative, normative, standardized, site-visited measures.

The FIRST STEP in thinking about middle school is thinking about kids ... thinking (systemically *and* emotionally *and* empathically *and* intellectually) about who they are, what makes them tick, how they got there, where they're going, why they are, why they're not, how they think, how they think about you, what they think about thinking about, what they're afraid to think about ...

AND, you really need to STOP here for a few minutes and think about this: Do you really believe all kids—every kid—can learn? Do you really make decisions based on "what's good for kids" or is that just lip service, a good phrase for Open House, and something that sounds good in an interview? If you're not there yet, that's fine—but admit it so you can progress.

Wait a minute!
Have YOU written anything yet? This is thought-provoking stuff only if you allow it to be. I hope you're not just flipping the pages. (Oh, by the way. If I am offending or intimidating you with these expectations OR if you just feel silly doing it — HOW DO YOU THINK THE KIDS FEEL SOMETIMES WHEN AN ASSIGNMENT ISN'T A PERFECT MATCH WITH THEM OR THEIR EXPECTATIONS?)

on mission statements

If you have to publish it or put it up on the wall, especially framed, then it's not your real mission nor is it everyone's collective agreed-upon mission. Mission is what you believe, what you do, what you say, and how you act in the most subtle of ways, how you react under pressure, and what you go to the proverbial line for.

Should we have them? YES.
A mission statement is the Preamble.

Mission statements are our core beliefs and our beliefs about core. They are what makes us tick after we think about the kids and what makes them tick. It's, as they say, the walk we walk, the talk we talk, and walking the talk. It's the "that's in line with middle school philosophy" and the critique that something "goes against middle school philosophy."

But, as noted, if it's not apparent in every action, every decision, every lesson, every project; if it's not apparent in the halls, the cafeteria, the gym, the music room, the science lab, or the library; if it's not taken advantage of in teachable moments with kids and adults . . . then it's not your mission.

("Self-evident truths" need to be evident)

**Middle school?
The successful middle school?**

Easy: just build the school around the kids, literally and figuratively.

That deems repeating:

JUST BUILD THE SCHOOL AROUND THE KIDS, LITERALLY AND FIGURATIVELY!

If you think about them all the time you don't need a next step; the rest just happens naturally.

P.S. and don't forget that the school (that you build around them) doesn't mean school building as we know it, necessarily. But if you must have a building, build it around kids: team areas (including science), a homebase, reduced traffic, reduced bells, room to grow, space to be creative and explore, and . . .

put the library in the middle and make sure everyone *uses* it, often.

OKAY,

are you with me? As you can tell, you are going to do a lot of the work here.

Work?

Thinking about .... That is the work of professionals.

Thinking about successful schooling. Thinking about culture. Thinking about middle school. Thinking about successful middle school culture.

(And reading between the lines and finding the clues and hints embedded throughout the text).

And then, constructing meaning out of all of it and figuring it out for yourself. (Now does this make sense?)

So, get out that highlighter, your post notes and your pen, and let's go at it!

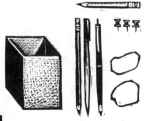

TIME OUT: In case I have lost you ...

In case I have lost you already, let me provide a left-brained view of where this is going. Now, if you didn't like doing proofs in geometry or solving logic problems, you may want to just skip this page — in the long run it doesn't matter — well, it does, but that's okay.

I will start with the proposition that everything is SUCCESSFUL SCHOOLING. You can use any phrase you want — effective schooling — quality schooling — restructuring — or the buzzword of the month. Bottom line? We want successful schools.

So, how do we (notice I didn't say "I" but rather "we") define successful schooling?

I. We start with some COMMON SENSE MIDDLE SCHOOL STUFF (research , information, and experience) related to successful schooling.

II. Then we move to CULTURE (it's all culture).

III. Then we go a bit more in depth and talk about CONSTRUCTIVE CULTURE. The constructive culture is actually what we're shooting for with the successful schooling (well actually it's democracy but that's pretty deep for the first chapter of any book on education).

IV. Then we move to analyzing CONSISTENCY in PRINCIPLES, PATTERNS, and PRACTICES (which is also what we're shooting for to define successful schooling). ("I thought he said we were shooting for culture...or was it democracy...or...")

V. Then we bring it all home with the principal and teachers and those who think about this in parts and in total.

GOT THAT?   *Successful schooling*   =   *common sense middle schooling.*
Successful schooling   =   *constructive culture.*
Successful schooling   =   *consistency in principles to practice from a constructive perspective.*

If successful schooling is the **what**, achieving consistency in principles, patterns, and practices is the **how.**

Well, actually it doesn't matter where you start for two reasons:

1) Everything is contingent upon everything else and it must all be consistent — so where you begin to think about it doesn't really matter.

2) None of this matters because all that matters is what YOU do with what you read and reflect and the meaning you construct from it. The most important features of this book are the pieces that stimulate thought, some consideration of what you do, and a little controversy.

Feel better? (Probably confused you more, right?) Well, proceed, please.

CHAPTER 2 Successful Schooling

or

How will we know when we're doing a good job, because as long as it's in middle school someone will be critical of our work?

Thinking about middle school — about successful schooling?

Let's start simple and practical.

Your school is successful:

- when every kid goes home and tells mom, dad, Uncle Al, Grandma Leah, or whomever, "School was great today";

- when there is a teacher in every classroom who knows, accepts, encourages, and cares about each student and who invites, expects, encourages, and causes learning in each student; and

- when kids, teachers, staff members, parents, and the community are learning, individually and collectively.

Period

What's the proverbial bottom line?

Learning — if the kids are learning, you'll figure out how to measure it and brag about it. (Research, data, and evidence are important, but they don't always have to be quantitative measures.)

And by the way, even the most "prestigious" universities have figured out how to review applications of students from high schools that do not compute GPAs or provide class rankings.

That's right — there are "prestigious" high schools in America that churn out Ivy League students without the heavy competition (but with a lot of hard work).

And there are hundreds — not dozens — hundreds of universities and colleges (with names other than Harvard and Prestigious U.) out there developing future leaders and successful citizens from high schools all around the country.

Learning and enjoying learning

And, there are hundreds and thousands of high school students out there who are NOT in the top 10% of their graduating classes who are quite successful by any measure you wish in those hundreds of universities (and other places, too).

And, guess what? They all went to a middle level school, some of which probably dealt with self-concept, exploration, and all that "hands-on learning" stuff right along with their academic rigor!

on self-esteem (the defensive response)

Let's get this one out of the way early. It starts with the premise that some administrators and a lot of parents just don't get it. They assume that the first time you utter those affective words: "self esteem" (a.k.a. *touchy-feely, self-concept, go-hug-a-tree,* and *the whole child*) you've become a no-competition— values clarification— making posters all the time—"hasn't read a book in two years"— grades don't matter—teacher.

Why? Someone tell me why the first time we mention that we are concerned about a child's self-esteem, critics naturally assume we are indoctrinating kids to "make peace, not war,"

burn the flag, and question authority? Why do they assume we are dumbing down the curriculum and holding back a child's academic growth? Help me with this one, please. Work is work. And poor teachers who don't assign or make appropriate decisions about quality work are probably pretty rotten at developing self-esteem, too! Self-esteem? Empowerment. A sense of "I belong here." Self-confidence. Feelings (yes, feelings) and behaviors of competence. Taking risks in learning

and discovery. Getting back on the bike when one falls—with adult encouragement.

Really, now. We're not talking about spending third period every day in pursuit of self-actualization. We're talking about developing an attitude of: "I can do this work." "I can get through this tough math problem." "I have something

on self-esteem (the rationale)

Now, let's not throw out the touchy-feely attitude of acceptance altogether. A technique used often by conference presenters is to ask participants to go out and talk to "non educators" in the hotel what they remember about junior high. The responses usually fall in two categories. The positive ones include field experiences and/or a teacher who was really motivating and accepting of kids.

The negative ones include peer pressure(s), feeling awkward and different, feeling left out, and/or a teacher who embarrassed them. Try it.

The story spread all over the school. 'Did you hear?' Mr. G. told Laura that her new hairdo looked like a beehive. She ran out of the room crying.' I remember it well. She was so humiliated. A throw-off sarcastic comment by an insensitive music teacher in 1965. Yet, here it is thirty years later—and I remember—

and I bet Laura does, too. I wonder if Mr. G. does? Probably not.

My best friend from junior high died a few years ago. The last letter I received from him keeps me on course, especially when I feel like I am about to sell out to the "school is not for social development" critics.

He wrote about the pretenses and the phoniness of junior high and high school. He'd "played the game" as he

to contribute in this class."
"I am a part of this team." "I can take a risk without worrying about being embarrassed" (okay, so that one's a stretch— no middle schooler EVER stops thinking about being embarrassed).

So, lighten up—remember, this was the defensive response

to be nobody but yourself,
in a world which is doing its best, day and night,
to make you like everybody else means to fight the hardest battle
which any human being can fight . . .
but never stop fighting.

— e. e. cummings

described it and that only made things worse.

Every time I think of him, I realize that if we could just . . . make folks a little more sensitive, a little more empathic . . . foster fewer put downs . . . take the complaints of picking on and teasing seriously . . . not tolerate bullies . . . let kids know that it's "okay" to just be yourself in our rooms, halls, schools . . . work on building self-confidence . . . help kids accept the necessary criticism after they blow a test listen . . .

Fortunately, most teachers, administrators, and schools are taking care of this by their very nature and capitalizing on the teachable moment.

Sadly, some aren't.

No one, especially an adult in a school, has the right to hurt a student's or an adult's feelings.

Period.

Self-esteem?

Just like any other topic related to successful schooling, this issue of self esteem is not an either-or thing.

One doesn't "do" self esteem anyway. It's there — like listening, engaging in dialogue, mutual respect, understanding.

It's the teachable moment. It's acknowledging the good try.

It's not allowing the put down from the third seat in the second row across the aisle.

It's not publicly humiliating a kid. It's pointing out a strength and developing a talent.

It's

— making sure the new kid who walks into your overcrowded room on the second day of school doesn't think it's her fault the class is overcrowded.

— pushing a kid to try harder with a tough question.

— making sure Tim has a lab partner when no one wants to sit with him.

— giving a student five extra math problems because you are saying "I know you can do this."

It's not

— saying "how can you not know where your father works?"

— reading the entire list of test grades to the class.

— telling the kids who get free or reduced lunch to "line up over here."

(And report card-focused parents, it's not *Four A's and a B. Why didn't you get that B up to an A?!*)

Are you beginning to figure out that this is not your ordinary text?

I was going to paraphrase that car commercial — you know —

"This is not your father's Oldsmobile."

Well, this is not your father's text on schooling.

The kicker is that this is probably a whole lot more like your grandfather or grandmother's text on successful schooling than your father's. We had a lot of right answers decades ago but didn't have the guts to stay on course!

Successful schooling?

An interview

Prin: *How do you develop trust with your students?*

Teach: I greet them at the door every day. I notice something special about them — anything — as I invite them in to learn. And I let them know I believe in them. There's something each student can do and we build on that. I respect them for who they are — not for who they're not. I listen to them, really listen.

Prin: *How do you decide what to teach?*

Teach: The kids! I know you probably expect me to say "the curriculum" but that's a given. My decision is based on matching the kids — one by one and all of them — with the curriculum and figuring out a way to arrange the pieces of the curriculum into the kids' interests, ideas, and discoveries.

Prin: *Can every student be successful in your classroom?*

Teach: Yes. I expect that every student can learn. I work hard not sending any messages that one student can't. No stereotypes of any variety. Once we let a student think we think that another is innately "smarter" or can do more, we reinforce every stereotype they see on TV, at home, and in the neighborhood. Now, would you like to discuss labels on kids?

Prin: *How do you define success for yourself as a teacher?*

Teach: High expectations of every student — not just in my class but that they have a bright future. An inviting "can-do" classroom. Respect for every student through my actions. Learning myself all the time. Hard work and having fun. That's success. The pedagogy — teaching techniques — that just comes over time. You've got to care about every kid. And, of course, if they're successful and growing, I am, too.

Prin: *So, Myron comes up to you and says, "I just can't spell. "What would you do?*

Teach: Look down his throat! When a kid says his or her throat hurts, do you prescribe medicine, give a shot, tell them to gargle . . . or do you look first? No two sore throats are alike — same goes with learning problems!

on professional growth

That's a two-parter:

first, the teacher as professional . . .

then the growth part.

PROFESSIONALS don't count hours, punch clocks, count days, sweat the small stuff, or label kids. They don't blame victims or society. Professionals understand that time is scarce, but they find it. They see individuals, not groups. They apply their knowledge and they keep abreast of everything. They immerse themselves in one thing, and then another, and another. They are growing. And they "own" their kids, just like family.

Do professionals have pressure points? Do they have limits of how much they can take? Are there class sizes that are really just too big? (overheard at a recent conference: "The research is out on the optimum class size. It's 'five less.'") Are there budgets that are just too small? Of course. But it's amazing how many find ways, protest loudly, and then get over it.

And, the message here, quite honestly, is for the leaders, the team leaders, the principals, the curriculum leaders, the superintendents and others in the crowd: most of the time it's our fault that a teacher is not behaving and believing like a professional. You either . . .
1) hired an assembly line worker to do think tank work, or
2) created conditions which allow him/her to count everything that doesn't move and stifle everything that does move — like kids — and learning.
(I put that in a list because otherwise those technical leaders wouldn't get it or wouldn't bother reading it).

And, the GROWTH part is simple. If a teacher thinks s/he knows all there is to know, then his/her class is not going to get any better because s/he is not. S/he may have it down to a science, but teaching is an art — and as for the science part, no two brains are alike, and that knowledge base changes every minute (in the real world). The technician works hard to do the same thing over and over and over to avoid flaws. Imagine an artist painting the same picture over and over and over.

Technicians start with nothing and develop products that are supposed to be the same. Artists (and educators) start with people and . . .

:-("Wait. What did he mean by that 'in the real world' crack?"

Well, we hope we are beyond our refusal to change the content of our course of study, but if we are so progressive that we change the content of our courses >>>>>> Why do we refuse to accept that the same knowledge explosion might apply to knowledge about TEACHING AND LEARNING as much as it does to technology and international diplomacy?

And, by the way, enough already on the knowledge explosion sound bite. We accept that the knowledge base in the real world doubles every (what's the latest) six months, three months, thirty days (haven't you had enough of that already)?

To paraphrase a well-known frowned-upon bumper sticker:
CHANGE HAPPENS! So stop talking about it and deal with it.

Think about it.

(That's an imperative sentence: YOU, the reader, think about it.)
So get out a pen and get defensive if you must ...but think about ...

Kids — early adolescents.

Adults — professionals, staff members, parents, community.

Knowledge.

Learning how to learn.

The future.

Change.

Relationships.

Successful schooling.

Culture.

ASIDE:
(I was always intrigued by "the aside" — when a Shakespearean actor [wasn't it Shylock who tried to justify his behaviors to the audience?] or Ferris Bueller would step outside of their scene, talk to the audience, and then jump back into the text.)

AN ASIDE on the "interactive" nature of this book: As I am sure you can tell already, as you read this book, you will discover some things about your teaching, your parenting, your learning, your school(ing), and yourself. You will also learn a few things about the author. As you read, we will agree on some items. We will disagree on others. I might even offend a few of you with my assumptions or assertions. (Might? We got past "might" several pages ago.) I may validate the feelings of other readers. One way or the other, you should have some things to think about.

Oh, and, if we are going to get to know each other, I plan to save you time figuring out where I am on issues that will emerge. I will put my thoughts out on the page (those are the "on . . ." sections). React, reflect, refute! And put yours out for yourself . . .

For example . . . let's get a few things out on the table now about successful schooling in relation to adopting new programs. It will also set the stage for some thinking about means and ends, systems, and technical and illusory schooling.

on programs

I don't do programs.
(I especially don't do programs with acronyms).

Programs come and go.

Programs are the latest innovation
that never stick.

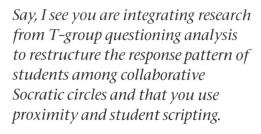

A program is throwing money
at a problem.

Programs are illusory.

Programs cause administrators and teachers to say
"I thought that was last year's thing."

Programs cause legitimate systems changes or new frameworks to be treated like,
well, programs, and they never become woven into the fabric of schooling
practices.

And, most importantly, we alienate some group when we do programs (or at least
labels), because individuals are either for a program or against it.

So, why set yourself up for failure by putting a label on something that half of
your students/parents/colleagues will be for or against? If it's that good, just do it.

*Say, I see you are integrating research
from T-group questioning analysis
to restructure the response pattern of
students among collaborative
Socratic circles and that you use
proximity and student scripting.*

*Naw, I just put 'em in groups and
give them a few problems to solve.
I wander around to make sure each
kid is working and taking notes.*

*Yes, but what do you call that?
Cooperative teaching? Collaborative
focusing? Or is it that new program,
that W.O.R.K. program?*

I call it . . . good teaching.

As for labels and especially
acronyms, think about one of the
acronyms in your school. Do you
know who named it? Do you
know what the initials mean?
Can the teachers teaching it
articulate the original rationale
for the program? Have new
teachers been 'trained' to use it? If
you answered
"yes" to all four of those questions
I will retract my statement — but I
don't expect too many letters.

Thomas Jefferson sat around with a few of his friends and wrote the Declaration of Independence. I am sure a few folks did the research, a few contributed to the conversation, and no doubt a few didn't keep up their end of the work. They all got the same grade, but each got individual attention and a unique place in history.

When Rosa Parks' feet were tired, she sparked a protest that changed the future (actually that's a myth — Rosa's feet may have been tired but she was tired, tired of discrimination). Martin Luther King, Jr. got together with Ralph Abernathy and a few other friends and mapped out a rather risky and courageous course that changed the nation. Dr. King made the speeches. Rev. Abernathy helped with the strategy. Many others spread the word. Thousands carried out the project. They all got the same grade; each achieved unique, individual success and satisfaction (even though not everyone in America quite got the message).

And sometimes everyone in the endeavor does not get the same recognition. Does the name Michael Collins ring a bell? His trio holds a milestone date in our technological history. Maybe a second member will help. Buzz Aldrin? Still stumped? The other is Neil Armstrong. Aldrin and Armstrong walked on the moon. Collins was in the orbiter etching his name in history with the thousands of other anonymous contributors on the ground.

Space flight, building skyscrapers, and county councils. Group planning. Would we know about Watergate if Woodward hadn't met Bernstein? Could Congress operate without subcommittees (Okay, forget that example). Middle schools without teams? Have you ever seen the awards for writers on the Emmys when the stage wasn't filled with creative minds and their collective awards?

How many texts do you use with only one author? Wasn't the Declaration of Independence the first collaborative, group project, interdisciplinary simulation in the country?

I call it school work and get away with it.

You call it cooperative learning and get the you're-dumbing-down-the-curri-culum where's-the-academic-rigor folks AND the no-federal-state-interference it-wasn't-like-that-when-I-went-to-school you're-doing-social-experiments-on-my-kids folks on your doorstep.

Now, be honest. How many times have you heard:

... you're using my kid to teach other kids,

... you're teaching to the middle/low end,

... you're giving group grades and my kid did all the work,

... you're reducing my kid's grades because so and so didn't do hers,

... you're doing away with competition,

... you're cheating my kid,

... ? !

Advice: Unless you adopt a bona fide program hook, line, and sinker; get trained in it; fit it in as a means to an agreed upon end; monitor your progress with it; and train the new folks ...avoid programs and avoid labels, too.

Successful schooling is not a program or label. Who created all the jargon and validated all the jargon in the first place? Isn't it all just school and good teaching? If we gave daily spelling quizzes and memorization of the Presidents an acronym, the back-to-the-basics crowd would be against it. Get rid of the labels and just teach kids and school.

SUCCESSFUL SCHOOLING? Simple. Kids reading and writing and painting and researching and singing... and... kids learning. Kids working. Those are the ends. The rest, including programs and projects, are means to that end (more on that later)

on programs and labels ... and tradition!

OR "The 'I had to walk five miles to school... in the snow... uphill... both ways' syndrome."

OK, what have we learned here?

Message #1.   **Avoid programs as separate entities.**

Message #2   **Avoid labels** (especially cute acronyms).

Message #3.   **Remember, nothing is either/or in middle school** (so why give it a name and the impression that it is THE only way)?

Message #4.   **Programs and other innovations are means to an end, NOT ends in themselves.**

Message #5.   **Programs and other innovations should "fit"** — they should be connected to existing systems.

Message #6.   **Don't mess around with some traditions!** Give homework, book reports, and weekly vocabulary quizzes. Teach kids how to make change (that always seems to come up on the talk shows — "the kid couldn't even make change") and make the kids memorize their times tables and the Preamble.

   Some programs are institutionalized, expected, traditional, and sentimental. And a little old fashioned self-disciplined hard work is good for every kid! Keep them in perspective (means, not ends), bite your tongue if you disagree, and pick your battles.

For the parents reading this, you may wonder if this isn't manipulative *middleschoolspeak*. No.

The programs you hear teachers discuss are well researched and the teachers (should be) well trained. If you hear a teacher say s/he is using "writers workshop" you should expect the teacher not only knows the process but that s/he thinks about it often and adjusts its application to each unique group of students.

For the teacher reading this, unless you ARE a purist and trained and practiced and professional at using a well-researched technique, PLEASE don't use the name at Open House or other discussions. These approaches are well researched. Homemade adaptations only give those who have studied for years a bad name.

There is nothing wrong with book reports, spelling tests, and reading the classics. The routine, self-discipline, clear expectations, good old-fashioned work, and predictable nature of them go a long way with many students. It's just that they are not ends — they are means along with numerous other learning experiences.

(Well, did you catch that - a "thinking about" statement.)

And, let's keep it all in perspective: our time tested, traditional, accepted-by-all features such as teaming, advisory, homebases, exploratory blocks, and others *are* programs, no more no less. It's just as problematic to think of them as ends as it is any other program.

READ THAT AGAIN.

(Principals, instructional leaders, and especially those of you on campuses who haven't been in a school for a while — READ THIS PAGE — it may be the most important one in the book).

This page is dedicated to my friend, George Melton.

George and I have been writing to each other on E-mail for about four years (we finally met each other in person after two years). George is one of the "granddaddys" of middle school, former middle school principal, former Associate Executive Director of NASSP, and a believer that everything should have a purpose, a meaning, and should be based on a keen understanding of adolescents and adolescence.

I f you don't understand the building blocks of middle school — learn them or stop using them. You're killing it for the rest of us. More on that later.

So, the questions are:

DOES IT FIT IN?

IS IT CONNECTED?

IS IT A MEANS TO AN END?

DOES IT STILL REINFORCE OUR PRINCIPLES ABOUT LEARNING AND TEACHING?

If the answer to these is "YES," then hang on tight to your program — you've obviously thought about it in context of the broader mission of your class/school.

If the answers are "no" — well, it's time to rethink them.

If your response is, "I am not sure" or worse than that, "I'd say 'yes' but our faculty doesn't see it that way," then it's time to put on the brakes and study middle school.

"Just like when I was in school"

Aliciea: Mom, I have like *soooooo* much homework. Like, not only algebra but I have to read like this ancient book.

Mom: *What book are you 'like' reading?*

Aliciea: *Great Expectations.* It's so lame. I like don't get it. And it's so totally boring with all this like old English stuff. I mean like who would actually like anonymously to be a benefactor, you know, like give money, can you believe it, to a teenager, right, you know?

Mom: *Oh, we read that (a Temptations medley plays in the background) when I was in school. Just work at it, honey.*

Those magic words...the key to successful schooling
AFTER we get past the real stuff:

"JUST LIKE WHEN I WAS IN SCHOOL!"

I still look for four-sided paper kites (good luck), use a mercury thermometer to check for fever on my biannual battle with a vacation (my body seems to know when I am taking a break and I get sick), and tell our son about how "when I was a freshman I had to use a slide rule to multiply pie are squared." (tee hee).

So, why fight it?

And, like you know, well, like...what's wrong with a little memorization, an old fashioned book report, OR HOMEWORK?

Cool.

BACK TO SUCCESSFUL SCHOOLING

What does all this have to do with success?

EVERYTHING.

Means and ends.

Fitting in.

Purpose.

or

Labels for the sake of labels.

Programs to "have one of those."

How would you know a successful lesson, class, room, school, team, "program," teacher, leader, administrator, student, book, model, project, idea, field trip, assembly, essay, lab experiment, sculpture, speech, master schedule, cafeteria, or group if you saw one?

Could you be found guilty by a jury of your peers for having a successful classroom? school? team?

Well?

Prove it!

on courage

What are you willing to go to the line for?
(I know. I shouldn't end the question with a preposition.)

Okay. For what are you willing to go to the line?

Anyway, that's it on courage ... no explanation needed.

Okay. I lied. One more thought.

If the answer to the question above is based on the development of kids, the principles of middle school, or the concept of professionalism, it's a worthy item for risk.

Figure out the rest.

Success?

"Well, it's an *effective* school."

"It's an *efficient* program."

"We have a *total quality school.*"

"It's a school that meets the state's minimum standards."

"It's a clean school with posters and slogans everywhere."

"The parents are happy!"

Effective, efficient, clean, happy?
Please.

Important? Yes.

The bottom line? No.

(A little confused? That's okay. The means and ends part comes up again, and again, and again.)

Is success contingent upon test scores? merit scholars? awards and rewards? parent acceptance? teacher evaluations? administrator approval ratings? state assessment team evaluations? absentee rate? drop out rate? suspension rate? number of headlines featuring positive aspects of the school? percentages of tax levy/bond issues votes? number of complaints at the main office? number of conventions attended? number of contests won? cleanliness of the school? amount of homework given? or just good PR?

On one hand, it's "all of the above." They all matter. It's just that some of them matter more to some folks than others. I suppose the first question to ask is "successful according to whom?" Your colleagues? The community? The board? The students? The superintendent? The media? And, don't forget, as the cast of characters changes so does the definition of success.

Advice: be sure to define success for yourself.

Do YOU know how YOU define success? Does your boss know how you define it? Do your parents/colleagues know your definition? Your kids? (And, here's a clue for you all — the walrus — < sorry, couldn't resist > seriously, your definition should focus more on what you believe and stand for rather than an advisory period, a shopping list of innovations, or a thirty-minute duty free lunch.)

Advice: figure out what you do when "they" change the rules on you. Do you play by their rules or do what you know is best for kids — every kid — all the kids?

Successful according to whom?

Start with YOUR definition based on your research and "thinking about."

Success begins somewhere up there with lofty educational principles and beliefs. It is defined by other elusive concepts such as student success, professional growth, and democratic principles.

Success is defined in terms of justice, responsibility, equity, meaningful work, and application of knowledge and skills.

Success is found in means and ends, and the appropriate relationship between them. But this is the stuff of the next few chapters.

First, consider success from your perspective and from a very practical perspective, then we'll get in to the heavy stuff.

(You may, of course, disagree, but this is my first book, so I will go out on a limb here).

Time to define success on your own. Another is that the only way one learns anything is to figure it out alone. So...

(Note: the rest of this page is blank for you to do some "figuring out on your own" - oh, those who remember *Teaching as A Subversive Activity* will recognize where I stole the idea.)

Success? Relationships!

We can investigate new methods of alternative assessments, school organizational patterns, approaches to literature; we can network, collaborate, and even commiserate as part of our professional routines; however, when Johnny, Antoine, Tara, Sam, Sarah, Carlos, and Tamika go home every day, the only thing that matters about *your* successful school is when mom or dad asks, "How was school today?"

(How *was* school today?)

A periodic "it was great" gets mom and dad through the year.

And beyond that ... "School? It was great, I really like the way we are learning history this year" will get notes sent to school (you know, the kind that you put in your "what a lousy day" folder so when a lousy day creeps up you read all of those notes for a recharge.)

And then there's the comment that pops up at the spring music concert: "Our daughter talks about you and your class all the time at dinner" or "so YOU'RE Mrs. So and So. Our son is so motivated. He's determined to be a scientist because of you." And better yet, the principal is standing right behind you. (Well, cut my salary in half, because I won't need it in teacher heaven!)

Of course, routine negatives (boring classes, kids not being challenged, lost in the shuffle students) will foster a note or comments at the concert, too.

Either way, this is the stuff of successful schooling.

Either way, your portfolio assessments, your workshop approach to writing, your TQM, and new cafeteria layout mean nothing. If they work, fine. Successful schooling starts with knowing kids and building relationships.

(Better say that again in case someone is skimming).

SUCCESS STARTS WITH KNOWING KIDS AND BUILDING RELATIONSHIPS.

(Principals, team leaders, and others should substitute "teacher" for "kids": Success starts with knowing your teachers and building relationships).

Inviting kids to learn. Expecting success. Anticipating bright futures. Liking the kids. Knowing the kids, one by one. Caring about each one. Challenging them to learn and grow. Modeling. Learning what makes each other tick. Empathy. Walk in my shoes. Get to know ME. Don't label or categorize me.

Success?
Growing teachers — professionals, reflective practitioners, Expectations that every student will succeed.
A teacher in every classroom who ...

on sarcasm

This one will leave lots of room for your comments because the message, adapted to a 70s expression, is simple:

SARCASM

IS NOT HEALTHY

FOR CHILDREN,

ADULTS,

AND OTHER LIVING CREATURES.

Plain and simple — there's always an ounce of truth (or more) behind a sarcastic statement — and kids know it. Listen next time someone makes a sarcastic comment about or to a student and ask yourself "could they *really* mean that? Bet your answer is "yes.")

(and "shut up" falls in the same category)

Self—esteem? (again)

"Al, great to see you today. How's the day going? It's going to be a tough class this afternoon. You better block out at least an hour for my homework.

"That's right, an hour, but I know you can do it. Say, I know you're interested in fairness so I am going to ask you to summarize section number two on rights for the class tomorrow. I thought a little advance notice might help. Think about that when we review today in class.

"Sure you can handle that. By the way, you got sixteen out of twenty on that quiz yesterday. What did you do to study those questions on the legislative branch? You got all seven of them right. Be sure to use the same technique when you study for the quiz Friday.

"That's right, another quiz Friday. Oh, have you met Ted? Maybe you and your buddies could sit with him today? Thanks, I knew I could count on you. Enjoy your lunch."

(By the way, the debate of professionals and lunch duty will never be resolved but I assure you that teachers in successful schools at least cut through the cafeteria periodically to talk with kids outside of the classroom setting.)

The point?

Content can be tough. Class can be tough. Homework can be tough. But we can still reinforce a kid's self concept and build success on success. How many times have we heard, "You got a 90. Let's see what you did wrong on those two five-point questions that YOU GOT WRONG." Just for once, try, "You got a 90. Let's see what you did RIGHT when you studied those topics and be sure you keep doing that when you study for the next test."

SUMMARY

This is where the chapter summary would usually be placed; however, if you're really thinking about middle school and successful schooling, the only summary that matters is yours. Read on to try to make some sense out of "successful schooling."

CHAPTER 3 The Challenge: Perspectives on Successful Middle Schools

Putting the Middle School in Perspective ...

or

"I'll bet in twenty years we'll still have five pound textbooks on top of desks that are lined up in rows for kids seven periods a day, five days a week, with summers off."

The history of education shows that every attempt to break out of the student-as-consumer-of-fact syndrome has been hindered by routine steps backwards "to the basics." Consider post 19th-century industrial era, post Dewey, post World War II, post Sputnik, post civil rights/sixties, post *Nation at Risk*. In each instance, the general public and leaders (all looking for quantifiable results to satisfy their constituencies and résumés) couldn't handle the vagueness of progress. They returned to the safety of the factory model cult of efficiency school.

Elementary schools and high schools are stuck in this cycle. A few isolated efforts at restructuring will not change the face of American education at those levels. Middle school, on the other hand, is safe territory, for now. Consider that successful schooling, school restructuring, and middle school are synonymous. Again? Successful schooling, school restructuring, and middle school are synonymous!

High school and elementary school are general concepts understood by most Americans. (I note Americans because of the dreadful practice which sorts students into career paths in most other countries.) Have you ever heard a teacher say, "That's against elementary school philosophy?" No need. It's understood. Have you ever heard an administrator say, "That's not what high school is all about"? No need. It's understood. The definition and meanings, both steeped in tradition, are understood by all.

Everyone "gets" elementary school and high school. And, that's the problem. Everyone is an expert because they were once a student. Consequently, when a school takes on a particular bent — "a Coalition school," "an Accelerated school," a military school, a "fight free" school, or a magnet school of some variety — folks begin to scream. (Which is yet another reason not to "do programs" or use labels.) That, by the way, explains why successful reform, restructuring, and change are so rare at those levels. Tradition. The entity that originated in the factory era has taken on a life of its own and now cannot be revised (but that's another book).

Middle school, too, is embedded with meaning. That meaning, however, is not tradition. Say "middle school" to most folks and a mind set is created. A set of beliefs comes to mind. Specific systems are considered. Practices that are "middle school" by their very nature are shared. Middle school is a process. It is not a landmark of our history.

Middle school IS reform. It is restructuring that sticks. When folks hear middle school, the expectation is "something a little different." (If it fails, by the way, as did the progressive movement, then we can forget about any progress in education for decades.)

PRINCIPALS READ THIS!

CAUTION: Among the real concerns of middle level leadership is that yesterday's progressive transition to middle school (that's right, and it's not an oxymoron — *yesterday's progressive* transition to middle school) is becoming institutionalized and stagnant and that it is being tampered with regardless of guiding principles.

The former concern of institutionalized middle schools results from leadership which isn't thinking about the "why?" of middle school. The means become ends. The purpose is long forgotten and now we do things for the sake of doing them.

ASIDE:
Change! Changing from tradition — from the past? Heck, most leaders work hard to make their schools not only like the past but mirrors of each other today for fear parents may perceive school 'a' to be better than school 'b.'

The latter concern of tampering results from teachers and leaders not knowing their roots. They not only ignore the "why?" and the intended ends, they adjust schedules and little systems to accommodate their current needs.

Which leads us to ...

"Don't throw out the baby with the bath water ... BUT GET A NEW TUB!"

What is particularly scary about all this (at least to folks like me who think a lot about kids and learning and staying in school and professional growth) is that middle school is falling into the same trap as elementary school and high school, as concepts. We've reached a point where kids talk about teams, explo blocks, interdisciplinary units, and advisory and most adults *don't* flinch and ask "what's a team?" Teaming? Simulations? "We've *always* done it that way."

What is particularly scary is that teaming, explo blocks, blah, blah, blah, have become traditional. The presenters talk about them as if they were the DNA of middle school. Most of the folks implementing them don't know their history, their rationale, or their purpose. It's "just the way we've always done it around here" and "the research says that good middle schools have these things."

What is particularly scary about all this is that we have institutionalized our ambitions for middle school into a nine month year, five day week, six to eight period day with core subjects, electives, and grades.

What is particularly scary about all this (oh, by the way, you can skip ahead to the section on "Why Middle School is At-Risk") is that we are embarking on another one of the "post-" dips in our history which means the year 2000 will most likely kick off another back to the basics movement.

So what's the point?

Think about it this way...
When change happens too fast to our institutions, someone invariably stands up at the meeting (PTO, Board, curriculum advisory, or some other) right after the "I didn't need this approach when I was in school and I turned out all right" statement is made and says: "I am not opposed to a few new ideas but let's not throw the baby out with the bath water."

And, they're right. The BABY is doing fine. So is the WATER. The problem for decades has been the TUB!

SAVE THE BABY! SAVE THE BATH WATER! GET A NEW TUB! That's what needs to be junked — elementary school, high school, AND middle school structures which cause us to compromise what we now know about kids, teaching, and learning!

What is particularly scary about all this is that we're institutionalizing teams and explo blocks, but we haven't touched the structure. "School" hasn't changed a bit. And that's culture. That's "the way we do things around here." And, when it's all said and done, we always go back to the ways we've always done things around here.

Fortunately, middle school doesn't count.

It's sort of like summer school. We have some freedom to pilot and explore, as long as we don't veer too far off the traditional course ... just like American elitism, partisan politics, and health/welfare/defense/space exploration reform.

Consequently, middle school is essentially not only a symbol of restructuring, it is a metaphor for truly successful schooling rather than an exemplar of it! (You may need to let that one soak in a minute.)

Imagine a corporate executive — or a high school principal — saying "we need some change around here ... I want this place to go through a process just like middle school!"

Now, one must be a student of story and metaphor to truly appreciate the dichotomy of that proposition. Metaphor? The skeptical view presents metaphors for schools as prisons (as the kids would have us believe), assembly lines (as we look at the stupidity of our schedules), hospitals, shopping malls, and factories. On the positive side, metaphors of the symphony, jazz bands, amusement parks, and gardens are also heard.

The power of metaphor is the common body of conceptual knowledge related to the metaphor. When I utter "symphony" every reader knows what I mean. Therefore, when I state that "symphony" is a metaphor for successful schooling it implies individuals with different instruments, learning individually and collectively, rehearsing, routines, warm-ups prior to play, individual practice, individual recognition, music of the whole, performance, traditional pieces, contemporary works, and on and on.

If we aspire for our schools to be successful, and we select the jazz band, the orchestra, or the garden as the metaphor, an image comes to mind. Middle school, as a concept, is in that category with the idealized jazz band or garden and elementary schools, high schools, and other arenas of education should aspire to be like middle school.

Middle school. Restructuring. Successful Schooling. The terms could be synonymous in spite of back to the basics sequels. So, could middle school be the metaphor for schooling to which we aspire pre-K through university? Individualization? Exploration? Core knowledge? Team approach? Homebase? Field experiences and hands-on learning? Buildings and schedules built around what we know about kids and learning and teaching? Respect for (student and professional) growth and development? Rite of passage? Empowerment? Flexibility? Professionalism? Reasoned change? Perhaps.

Wouldn't that be something if... ? Wouldn't it be something if we walked into a restructured high school and someone complimented the faculty stating, "Wow, this is just like middle school!" — and everyone understood?

Let's Get on With It
or
"Whodunit"

ASIDE: Growing up, I loved doing those logic puzzles. Five people were taking the 9:52 a.m. train to New York. Three women. Two men. Two had black hair. One loved baseball. Four of them had never been on an airplane. Their names were Lee, Stacy, Mike, T., and Butch. The train stopped halfway to New York and Mike got off. The question: which of the passengers wearing a brown hat attended the Yankees game the day before, and who won?

I loved geometry. One of the highlights of my freshman year. Logic. Proofs. More than one way to solve the problem and the fun part was getting there, not the answer.

I have been fascinated and influenced reading everything by R. Buckminster Fuller and have recently tried to understand chaos. Deming has been an influence, too.

Consequently, when I write, think, plan curriculum, design workshops, or visit a school, there is a network of thought that eventually all comes together, like reading a mystery ... or watching a movie with multiple intertwined plots.

The brain intrigues me (and it amazes me that there are over a million of us teachers out there and probably none of us can tell you too much about how the brain works or how learning occurs – which is probably why we gravitate to rote memorization, right/wrong answer tests, and quantifying everything and not being able to defend our position as professionals).

By now you have picked up on several clues in this pursuit of the successful middle school and "making it happen" in middle school. The clues are dropped throughout the text.

As you proceed, you will continue to follow, I hope, the train of thought and the logic that will take us from the concept of successful schooling to successful middle schooling, to how leaders (not administrators — leaders — administrator leaders, teacher leaders, staff development leaders, parent leaders — leaders) "make it happen" in school.

And, like any mystery, thinking about and learning from the clues and sub-plots is as meaningful as solving the crime! So enjoy.

By the way — read between the lines, above the lines, behind the lines, as well as the actual lines. And don't get confused. There is no linear, sequential answer because it's not a linear, sequential (research) problem.

Oh, don't forget, several clues have been dropped already.

One More Way to Look at It (and a clue)

As a preview and hint, consider that all schooling is culture and that successful schooling is grounded in the characteristics of a constructive culture. (*Whoa, a 'constructive' culture - where did that come from?*) Middle school, by its very nature of principles and embedded systems is constructivist. (*I'm going to lose my readers here if I'm not careful*). Through poor leadership or attacks by the evils that lurk from beyond, the middle school can become technical or illusory (*definitions of these categories of culture are forthcoming*).

Before you run and hide from what sounds like a lot of philosophical jargon that comes from a dissertation (*hey, everyone's first book has to include something from their dissertation*), please know that all of this "culture stuff" applies to every classroom, every unit of study, every team and team meeting, as well as every school.

Stick with me. If it gets rough, I'll be right here to take care of you.

CHAPTER 4   Common Sense: The Middle School

A Pseudo-Case Study: Middle School

I t's around 8:00 a.m. (I don't wear a watch so "around" is the best I can do.) The cars are pulling up in front of school. One bus has arrived. Carlos has been sitting in the cafeteria since 7:00 when his mom dropped him off on the way to work. If he hadn't come with her he would have to board his bus around six, in the dark, in a neighborhood where one doesn't stand at bus stops in the dark, morning or night. He's been watching the news and doing some homework. Now he and his friends have switched over to Sports Center and his math book is in his back pack.

Dr. H. (okay, yes, this is based on a true story, only the names have been changed to protect the not so innocent) is outside with the first of too many cups of coffee, greeting kids as they get out of the cars. He knows as many of the parents as he does the kids and occasionally holds up traffic to chat with one of the moms or dads. (Hometown-boy-now-principal so

some of the parents are former classmates or neighbors). One of the buses from the city (desegregation program) arrives in front of the bus from the immediate area. The kids blend together on the way down the sidewalk with the few roller bladers who braved the cold, the walkers, the public transportation riders, and the few remaining skateboarders. Once on the sidewalks, grades, grade levels, gender, race, and ages don't seem to matter much. Kids!

Mr. S. walks outside just to talk. He is one of the most energetic teachers anyone has ever met. He checks to see if a few kids did their homework and applauds those who have. "Hey man," (he always starts conversations with the principal "hey man") "we're going to be out back in the garden — the kids are laying out their string plots. Hey, thanks for stopping by Saturday." (Who else but a fanatic pair of science teachers show up on Saturdays with their kids to 'do' mulch?)

A few more cars pull up as the bell rings to let the kids know it's okay to leave the cafeteria and front hall. (Sorry, I just can't accept the "wait outside in freezing cold weather just so we're not liable" approach to management.) Most disperse to their lockers and a few linger in the cafeteria. One group is still seated at a table with their counselor. She always manages to drop in during the morning to check on kids and get a feeling for "what's up." These teachers are not strangers to the cafeteria and halls before, during, and after school.

One parent stops on the way out to talk with Dr. H. She's just attended an I.E.P. for her child who has a learning disability. She compliments the school for responding so well and for the attendance of *all* her child's teachers at the meeting. It wasn't always that way and she had been among the most vocal criticizing Dr. H.'s defensiveness on the issue. (See, this is not totally self-indulging.)

Dr. G. sticks her head out the door. "I gotta dash but be sure to drop by today. The kids did solar ovens. Dan's is remarkable! He thinks he can cook muffins!"

The one minute drop-everything-and-get-in-the-room bell rings and the kids scatter. (Why have a warning bell that rings five minutes before the class? Five minutes to a thirteen year old equals three conversations, a note in the locker, and a trip to the bathroom to see if the mirror is still there, one more conversation, and three math problems completed. A one minute warning makes kids fly!) Most make the last second dash to avoid a tardy. Julie, an eighth grader, calls out to Nicole, "See you in band. Write me." ("Write me" as if she were leaving for Europe). They're on different teams so they only have classes together in arts and P.E. Sean and Mac stop their conversation about the latest printing of baseball cards and nod good bye to each other with typical twelve-year-old male indifference. "Later, man." "Yeah."

David dashes toward the door, glances at the reminder board next to the door, and makes a u-turn to get his permission slip out of his back pack.

Miss E., seventh grade, is standing at her doorway greeting kids. "Loved your essay, Nicole." Most of the kids are empty handed except for their coats which they hang on the rack Ms. M. had put on the wall last fall. They don't have first period in her room. Neither do any of the students in the adjacent rooms from their team but they all start their day there.

Meanwhile, three students fly into the office, drop off their roller blades in the closet (they don't fit in lockers), take their tardy slips and head upstairs. A parent walks in, "I'm his 'excused tardy.' My fault he's late" and departs with a kiss on the forehead for his not-as-embarrassed-as-you'd-think son. Dr. H. begins the announcements knowing full well that no one is listening. And the day begins.
All students start the day in

homeroom. This year the traditional schedule has sixth and eighth graders starting the day in a core (team) class. Seventh graders' first period is either arts, foreign language, or P.E., however, they physically start the day in their first core classroom — just like elementary school. Consequently, the start of the day homeroom is the first core team teacher the student has rather than an arbitrary "advisor" assigned by the alphabet.

Seventh graders go to their second period classroom to start the day. They all have P.E., orchestra, band, or a rotating arts block the first period of the day. Sending seventh graders to their first core classrooms allows the arts and P.E. teachers time to set up and students a way to start and finish the day "at home" with their core teachers, their lockers, their teammates, and assignments posted. The students settle in as the bell rings and the announcements begin. They visit or talk with each other. Their teachers remind them of what they'll need for class when they return.

By 8:35, eighth graders have begun their lessons. A quick walk through the halls reveals science labs unfolding, English classes beginning the mini-lesson prior to their Writers' Workshop, math students working mental math problems flashed on the overhead, and social studies classes tackling current events. The special education resource teacher dashes into the math class late from wrapping up the I.E.P. but ready to work with students in the classroom the entire period. The librarians set up materials and review their notes for the eighth graders due to arrive.

Still at 8:35, the sixth graders are tucked away in the ground floor or "the garden level" as they describe it to settle into their day. After the announcements, they get into their day methodically. Their rooms are filled with activity everywhere. They will be with their homebase teacher all morning with the exception of their hour in physical education and music block. The sixth grade does not use a "regular period" schedule. Their P.E.

classes are only a half hour, because they do not "dress out" for P.E. (Why should an eleven year-old be asked to change clothes in front of forty peers, involuntarily?) Students continue to copy the daily vocabulary, homework assignments, and responsibilities for the day off the board and begin working on their projects.

And now, at 8:35, seventh graders are dismissed to their real first period, and their core teachers meet in a classroom to begin their team meeting. The counselor drops into one meeting, unscheduled, to provide an update on a student. The resource teacher sticks her head in the door to see if she can steal five minutes to a resounding "no." It's not that the teachers are insensitive to her students' needs. It's that they have been working aggressively to stick to a format that gives them time to work on curriculum connections which they are determined to accomplish on this day.

Sixth and eighth graders are well into their lessons, while seventh graders

enjoy bounding out to the fields past the sixth grade classrooms, reciting a greeting to their teacher, taking out their sketches, tuning their strings, and blaring out that unstructured necessary band warm-up. And the day has begun.

It is now 9:30. The eighth graders are half way through their morning class (singular: class). Their teachers decided to go with double periods for the next two weeks, two subjects a day instead of four, alternating days. Since all the kids are on team, they have a common space, and they have two blocks of time they can reschedule until the proverbial cows come home and no one would know it. The only parameter from "the office" is that they know where to find a student if needed.

Sixth graders are winding up their first hour in either math/science or language arts/social studies. There are two person teaching teams in sixth grade. (No sixth grader should have to work with eight adults in a day.)

The seventh graders are coming in from physical education, putting instruments away in band and orchestra, and cleaning up in arts block classes.

Danny comes in from the soccer field with just enough sweat to necessitate washing up. The coaches only require that the students wash up, showers are optional. Since the curtains were put up in the boys showers, showers have increased. Similar to the thoughts above, no middle schooler should have to stand naked in front of other middle schoolers (literally or figuratively).

The seventh graders return to core class areas. A bell sounds. Sixth graders depart their area for music and P.E. Eighth graders never budge. At no time during the day are any two grade levels of students in the halls.

And, the day proceeds.

Constructing Meaning from a Pseudo-Case Study

Okay, time for some practice. Get out your marker again, Go back to the case study and begin to highlight the revealing points. They're everywhere.

Some are very obvious. For example, the eighth grade team's decision for block scheduling allows for alternate schedules and gives teachers control over time.

Some are obvious. For example: sixth graders do not take showers, every student starts the day in a core classroom (not class but the actual room), and kids on different teams can have arts and p.e. classes together.

Then there are points that are not so obvious. For example, did you catch the part about the student waiting inside the building even though there was no administrator stationed in the cafeteria? the part about the one minute bell? the part about the teacher at the door? and the part about the day's lesson written on every chalkboard?

It's all instinct and decision making, based on what we know and believe about kids, curriculum, and learning — and what we bring to the party, well, instinctively.

Give it a try. Remember, if you have questions the E-mail address is up front (p. 8)! Better yet, talk it over with a colleague.

And, if you are serious about thinking about middle school and the meanings in this book, come back to this section after reading the entire thing and see what else you discover (about culture, relationships, change, and communication).

Finished thinking about the case study?

Well?

Think about it.

(If you look at the word 'matters'
enough times you begin to wonder
if it's really a word that means anything.)

What matters is:

— knowing eleven-year-olds and fourteen-year-olds,
— thinking about every detail,
— going with your "gut feeling,"
— having a reason for what you do.,
— reaching out with sincerity, empathy, and reason,
— having a method to your madness,
— not getting so caught up in what you do that you think it's an end in itself;
— everything matters.

What matters is:

— having great ideas.
— that the practices fit into some logical explanation or some system of the school,
— that the practices and those systems reflect what you know and believe about
middle school kids, middle school teachers, and successful middle schooling,
— that those beliefs and practices reveal your thoughts
about the development of youngsters,
— that those beliefs and practices reveal your thoughts about work, knowledge,
relationships, and connections in schools, successful schools.

What matters is:

— greeting kids and parents at the doors.
— keeping 500 kids out of the hall at the same time.
— giving teachers the authority and flexibility to switch
their own schedules and other things that really matter.
— having the assignments on the board, in the same place, every day.
And,
What matters is that nothing we do matters in isolation,
but everything we do matters to everyone else - whether it's in isolation or not.

(Oh, by the way - notice anything about the three sections
of "what matters?" Here's a hint: Principles. Patterns. Practices.)

Middle school is reform.

("Oh, did I mention that before?" he said with no apology for redundancy.)

It is a prime example of restructuring. It exemplifies the concept of paradigm shift

(Ok, it wouldn't rock the Richter Scale, but it would get on the ten o'clock news).

Simply, we think differently about middle level education today than we have historically. It is generally (not totally) accepted that we now think about educating kids, the broader goals of education, not just teaching subjects at the middle level. *That's* the stuff paradigm shifts are made of.

I think it is too soon to tell, but history will probably show the reforms of the post-*Nation At Risk* era, both private and public initiatives, to be short-lived. America 2000, Goals 2000, RJR Nabisco award winners, corporate schools, and others will thrive, temporarily. Other well-touted financial plans of privatization have already failed.

On the other hand, there is a reform that was based on "who are the kids?" rather than "let's look at the scores" and it seems to be working: middle school.

And if it sticks, WHY is it so successful in its implementation?
If not, the critical question will be "WHY was it at risk?"
Either way, so what?

ASIDE: If middle school has the potential for a place in educational history as a "reform that stuck" – and it doesn't work – then we are all in for some dark educational days ahead, along with public education and democracy as we know it. And that's the truth! (Yes, I know that was mentioned previously, too. Please, think seriously about it).

Middle Schools, Change and the Future

We must pause for a moment and recognize that middle schools are only a step in a lengthy sequence of educating America. We must also recognize that the development of middle schools has a place in the history of education and that the "movement" is as vulnerable to societal and educational forces as the schools of the industrial revolution, the schools that responded to Sputnik, and to *A Nation At Risk*.

CHANGE!

Some schools just don't understand what it's really all about. They try to convince folks they are successful with their awards, displays, contests, rewards for walking and not chewing gum at the same time, reading the classics, sorting kids, and an alphabet soup of acronyms of isolated programs. And when anyone suggests a change, they respond with that all-encompassing defensive postulate that "it's against middle school philosophy."

Hey - where's the beef?

Others trouble themselves with moving too far away from tradition, even traditional middle school.

Pay attention — most Americans like tradition, need structure, and will allow you to take changes only so far.

Still others have institutionalized their successes. Their 1980s philosophy, approach to teaming, and interdisciplinary units served children well, but innovations in scheduling, grouping and regrouping, curriculum modifications, and technology don't seem to have a place in their "tried and true" approach.

"Have you looked at your mission, your guiding principles, and where education in general (not just middle school) is heading? Are you still on course?"

Others have proverbially "tweaked" the systems and programs so much that they no longer resemble nor, more importantly, address the same principles as originally intended.

"Have you looked at your mission, your guiding principles, and where education in general (not just middle school) is heading? Are you still on course?" (Yes, I know that's the same paragraph.)

And hundreds of others have found the balance — they respect change — they respect their communities — they understand kids — they stay focused on their genuine mission — they respect research and what they observe — they neither rest on their laurels nor change for the sake of change — they proceed with confidence, professionalism, and enjoy every day of school!

Why Middle School Works

Why does middle school work?

Enough doom and gloom "if middle school doesn't stick." It works and will continue to work if we pay attention and have the courage to go with the kids. So, why does it work and why is it so important to preserve?

1. Middle school doesn't count.
2. Middle school counts more than anything.
3. Respect for development - it's a good place to grow up.
4. Feet on the ground - literally and figuratively!
5. Teacher as learner
6. There are no final answers, no traditions, and most people have horrible memories of junior high.
7. There are no final answers, no traditions, and some people have wonderful memories of junior high.
8. Middle school teachers and middle school leaders are always thinking about ...

1. Middle school doesn't count.

...and the kids know it. Elementary students will do anything (usually) to please their teachers and moms and dads. High school students will do anything to improve their GPA. It all counts for college. Middle school? The credits don't count. Just show up and you pass. Even the most intrinsically motivated students know they can lay back just a bit and even experiment not doing homework. And even the most intrinsically motivated students inexplicably do lay back. Oh, and there's the social pressure that tends to supercede everything.

As for counting people and things in middle schools ... honor rolls; credits for promotion to ninth grade; counting how many paragraphs, pages, and classics; test scores; drill/skill computer software; and "having one of those" middle school things like advisory or explo blocks. Little competitive high schools in middle school clothing.

Please.

So what? The ones who do work, the ones who are successful, know their place in the scheme of things and just go about their business researching, discovering, exploring, digging, reading, writing, painting, climbing, experimenting, motivating, and creating, and yes, measuring when and how appropriately.

Unsuccessful schools are those that patronize the students and parents in one of two ways: 1) those that promote dozens of unconnected programs, incentives, bribes, and other gifts for doing what is expected anyway to motivate and "fix" kids, or 2) those that categorize and label students and thrive on traditional, rote, measurable lessons. The unsuccessful schools know the kids know that it "doesn't count" and then proceed to teach and treat school the same way. Those who write off the lack of student effort as "well, it's just middle school" deserve the bad reputation and criticism they get from the high schools and parents. Successful schools respect the kids, the age, the social issues and accept the challenge of reaching and teaching every student. Some schools work harder. Some just work less. The good ones work smarter.

2. Middle school counts for everything.

Peer pressure. Decreased parental involvement. Greater mobility and independence. Peer pressure. Changing friendships. Changing bodies. Changing self-concept. Adjustments to tougher curriculum. Parents not understanding (nor remembering) adolescence and adolescents. Influences of substance abuse. Academic pressure. The "hurried child" syndrome.

So what? Being between eleven and fifteen years old may be no more (but certainly no less) as intense as the high school and college years, but it is certainly the most misunderstood. It is also a critical springboard for success in those upcoming high school and college years. Middle school is the fork in the road for one's reputation, academic path, academic habits, and self-concept.

And let's face it. We may or may not do much to accelerate the learning of a "bright" going-through-puberty but-Mom, it's-not-cool-to-be-smart adolescent, but if we don't do everything we can to keep the already unmotivated and unsuccessful from losing all motivation and confidence, they're lost. And if we don't provide the balance between limits and freedom, pressure and motivation, and between inspiration and burnout, we may lose more than a few. Middle schools work because they *have* to — and most professionals take that pretty seriously.

3. Respect for development — A good place to grow up.

Middle school folks respect that eleven years old is eleven years old. They know that fourteen is not twenty-four in the work force. They know that middle school is a good place to grow up. How often have you heard a middle school parent say, "Why don't you grow up?" What better place to grow up? A place where the adults respect who you are for how old you are and that no two of you have matured alike anyway and that it's okay to be a kid and still work hard, do homework, and complain about vocabulary quizzes!

So what? Simply, middle schools work because "middle school knows kids."

4. Feet on the ground — literally and figuratively!

Middle school is where kids begin their toughest stage of development with their feet on the ground, literally and figuratively. Somewhere during sixth or seventh grade, somewhere around the ages of eleven or twelve or thirteen (or fourteen or fifteen) these guys enter puberty and all the other changes we know and hear in every presentation occur. Think about that one.

So, we've got these kids in school. They are changing relationships with their families. They are changing interests and hobbies. They are packing up the baseball cards and teddy bears and replacing them with the latest hard rock or rap CDs. They are ready to save the environment, protest the use of styrofoam at the local fast food restaurant, and complain about the injustice they face with teachers, administrators, parents, or peers. They refuse to wear helmets or seat belts, and they cross the street only when it says "don't walk." And yes, Mom, they would walk off a cliff if a peer did, too.

They have fears but think they can survive anything. They'll try almost anything. They don't care about grades but they'll study hard. They'll do anything for a teacher who knows about them and cares about them and nothing for their parents. They'll read any note you leave them, as long as you tape it to a mirror, any mirror. And, they will produce some of the most remarkable research projects, thought-provoking solutions to the world's problems, and some of the most

creative complaints about algebra teachers who never seem to explain it well enough.

Well, some of them. We have to be careful NOT to label the entire group with the typical, predictable, traditional middle schooler, early adolescent description because no two are alike. As a matter of fact, some parents wish their kids would display a few more of those resilient, superman syndrome characteristics.

So? "Who else would put 1,000 of these kids in one building for a seven hour stretch and attempt to teach, feed, and protect them but middle school teachers and administrators?" That's why it works!

We think about it all the time, and we understand.

Well, we take these kids during the period of their lives when they are going through the most physical, social, and emotional changes — and we put them in a bigger different school with new kids and new teachers

and new rules and new ways to organize their day and new expectations. HUH? Does that really make sense?

(There's nothing wrong with a K-8 school — no transitions!)

But, we ARE smart about all this because we make the changes that we can control (the building, the rules, the teachers, the expectations), and we introduce those in fifth or sixth grade BEFORE all the physiological and psychological changes kick in!

We put their feet on the ground, literally and figuratively, in the middle school before they grow.

The only thing that is normal is that nothing is normal.

5. Teacher as learner.

By the very nature of the middle school, teachers are learners, respected as learners, and are growing continually. There are varied avenues for teachers to grow and lead —

on the team, in the subject area, co-curricular activities, special projects, school governance, bridging elementary and high school teachers, and other opportunities. Middle school teachers cannot go through a day without thinking about kids and how kids learn, about content, and about how to motivate the kids to learn the content! This thinking occurs on a scheduled basis, an unscheduled basis, and in teachable moments.

So? It's simple: great middle school teachers know they don't know it all!

6. There are no final answers, no traditions, and most people have horrible memories of junior high.

Why does middle school work? There are no final answers, no traditions, and most adults have horrible memories of junior high. (It was worth repeating). So, we can do whatever we want and it's got to be better than the way it was last week, last year, or "the way I remember junior high" (as long as the kids have homework and complain that "it's hard"). Adult's memories of junior high recall boring, tedious classes with uncaring teachers.

And, for too many there are emotional, social scars that will never go away. Friends and no friends. Being popular and not. Looking in the mirror. Puberty. Come on.

That is why there are parents who attend Open House and marvel at our efforts. They state wish they could go back to school with this wonderful, caring faculty. They know there are adults who know their kids well at school and those adults help nurture relationships, lab partners, caring about each other, and even mediation when necessary. We ARE doing a very good job of attending to kids and curriculum. And that's significant progress for most who have negative memories of junior high.

7. There are no final answers, no traditions, and some people have wonderful memories of junior high. Why does middle school work? There are no final answers, no traditions, and most adults have wonderful memories of junior high. (It was worth repeating, too.)

Again, there are no final answers. The age, the being, and the curriculum are too disparate and ever-changing to be locked into research-based acceptance or traditions. As for the mem-ories, regardless of the academics, of which many adults still have few, junior high was a period of making new friends, of getting involved in causes, and growing up. First kisses and breaking up; passing notes and the first party; the Beatles, the Temptations, or Led Zeppelin — the music doesn't matter but the memory does — sports teams and reading real books. For many it was an okay time if not a memorable one.

And in retrospect, many begin to

And in retrospect, many begin to realize that some of their classmates were learning disabled, some had troubled families, some were going through tough times, and some didn't do all their homework — but it didn't seem to matter on the surface. We just all went to school, and we all survived. Some did well and went on to do well. Others didn't do so well but went on to do well. And when looking back from the twentieth year high school reunion, it didn't matter much anyway. But learning took place — there were great teachers — and there was room to grow up.

8. Middle school teachers and middle school leaders are always thinking about ...

Leaders of culture and learning are thinkers, not managers.

Leaders (administrators, teachers, parents, kids) in successful schools think first about kids and second about the professional growth of the adults and a whole lot about systems after that.

Teachers in successful schools think about kids. They also think about their professional growth, about innovation, about what works, about what didn't work, about planning, and about 100 other things each day. They have reasons for what they do besides "it worked last year." Reflective practice is not new to middle school teachers. That's why we have team meetings, study groups, professional journals, and walks at lunch time. And that's why any successful school is successful.

Help wanted:
Motivated, caring, nurturing, creative, scholarly individual able to coordinate and communicate with colleagues of similar description and able to inspire, motivate, and listen to early adolescents and their parents! Oh, and be willing to color outside the lines, because there are none. That's why middle school is successful.

on one of a hundred or so reasons
why middle school teachers are rather special

A common theme of the literature on educational reform is that these large cycles of reform and reaction have had little effect on the way teachers teach, the way students are expected to learn, and the way knowledge is defined in the schools. (1987, Richard F. Elmore, Reform and the Culture of Authority in Schools.)

— in *Educational Administration Quarterly, Vol. 23 ,*No. 4 November 1987, p. 61

Middle school teachers *are* immersed in middle school reform whether they choose to be or not. How can one not be involved in thinking (usually subconsciously) about successful schooling when having to focus on a very unique age group of students, a complex curriculum, and a spectrum of students' academic abilities and interests? The "reform" must come naturally. Simply, one does not use last year's lesson plans to teach this year's kids in middle school! If Elmore's assessment is accurate, then perhaps he needs to look at middle schools and transfer what works to all those other reforms!

ASIDE: and why some middle school teachers aren't so special

For those of you

...who prefer to teach in isolation,
... who refuse to switch your room to be next to others on your team (or don't understand why that's important),
...who think it's all about convenience for adults,
...who think it's about having an extra planning period,
...who continually make sarcastic comments about "the range of the strange,"
...who think it's "my way or the highway,"
...who think every twelve-year-old can sit in a chair for forty–six minutes without talking, leaning, or fidgeting,
... who think it's only about subjects and content,
... who think that content and skills don't matter,
... who continue to publicly humiliate students,
... who expect kids to learn organizational skills on their own,
...who are totally inflexible and won't score or even read or acknowledge a test because the kid didn't follow your directions, and.
..who think it's all about control, power, and authority,

...do the kids and your colleagues and yourself a favor and get out of middle school!

on middle school criticism

Middle level education, middle schools in particular, will always be under attack by some group. Middle schools are just as at-risk of failure and dropping out as their students, and perhaps, developmentally for the same reasons. But just like parents of thirteen year olds, the adults in charge will just have to face up to that. Some will get it, some won't.

I tire of the arguments for academic rigor and about "dumbing down" the curriculum. I tire, too, hearing of middle school teachers and activities who and which treat middle schools as those incapable of rigor and challenge. (Perhaps in our defensiveness we need to do a better job of listening and looking in the mirror because many of those complaints ARE legitimate.

I have seen too many projects and posters where kids went through the motions and *don't* have a clue about substance or who weren't challenged to apply new learning). Projects, performances, presentations, and group activities are essential WITHIN a system which insures quality research, homework, and communication of learning. If we allow our teachers and students to perform work only on the surface, without sophisticated understanding of the content, we are guilty of all of which we are accused.

I tire, too, of high school students and parents criticizing middle school for all the reasons regularly heard. (Short term memories, I guess.) Find a high school kid who says s/he worked as hard as s/he could because academics were at the top of his/her list every day in middle school, and I will show you a nose growing.

On the other hand, middle school IS at-risk of failure. Middle school "at-risk"? Take a healthy, happy, growing youngster. Detach her from the norm. Take away her hope. Infuse her with toxins, non-nutritious foods, and unhealthy practices. Disconnect her from learning. Disrupt her sense of purpose. Allow the community to deny its responsibility in her development. Take away her sense of "belongingness" and membership. Take her off course of healthy development. The result? A disengaged, child at-risk of academic and social failure.

The school is no different.

Take a healthy, happy, growing school. Detach it from the norm. Take away its hope. Infuse it with toxins, unhealthy practices. Disconnect it from learning. Disrupt its sense of purpose. Allow the community to deny its responsibility in the school's development. Take away its sense of "belongingness" and membership. Take it off course of healthy development. The result? A disengaged, school at-risk of academic and social failure.

Eleven Reasons Why Middle School Is At Risk of ...

(At-risk? At risk of what? *At risk of failure.*)

Are we in danger of losing our momentum and getting back to tracking kids into basals and rote lessons to "whip them into shape" for high school? Or, are we still on a positive path of our schools' development? Why are middle schools "at risk"?

Top Eleven Reasons Why Middle Schools Are At Risk of Failing

1. Leadership that doesn't understand early adolescents, restructuring, and ACADEMIC RIGOR.
2. Our instant gratification quick fix society mentality.
3. We've stolen the innocence from kids.
4. The Conservative Right, Parents of the 60's, & the Liberal But Probably Not Left.
5. There are no final answers, no traditions, and most people have horrible memories of junior high.
6. 90s early adolescents, baby boomer parents, and baby boomer leaders.
7. Oldest children.
8. The hurried child get-my-kid-in-Harvard we're-way-behind-Japan syndrome.
9. Teachers who still do subjects, not kids.
10. Tampering with systems, the boiled frog syndrome, "does it fit?" and "so what?"
11. Puberty.

---

1. Leadership that doesn't understand early adolescents, restructuring, and ACADEMIC RIGOR.

Middle school folks are unique. I once had a teacher comment to me that he knew I was committed to middle school professionally but didn't know I practiced it as a religion. Well, as a staunch advocate of separation of church and state (that's another book) I suppose there's a particular irony to that statement, but - he was right. How can one think about middle school without mission, passion, and investment?

You have to know the kids. You have to understand change and restructuring. You have to have strong, firm, unwavering principles and beliefs. You have to take risks.

Junior high is easy. Content driven curriculum, tracking, grouping, gifted programs, and bells are easy. Rewards and punishments to prove your authority and formula-driven discipline are easy. Symbolic, public displays of discipline and accomplishments to illustrate you're doing your job are easy. Completing checklists for supervision of instruction is easy.

Middle school is a challenge. It means assuming responsibility. It means being accountable. It means pitching the handbooks, guide books, formula approaches, teachers' guides, and anything else that is teacher/administrator proof (except the safety manuals) and making tough decisions. It means having a firm set of principles and beliefs and the courage to go to the line for both (as opposed to changing them every time the wind changes direction or the phone rings with an unhappy parent on the other end).

And, it means knowing kids.

Academic rigor? No problem with that. This is school and school should be hard work! Push kids! Give a lot of homework! Stretch the curriculum! Reading and more reading! Sweating over tough problems. Hard work! Self-discipline! Persistence! Kids on task! These should be part of the daily routine - and if they are not the school is not doing its job (and perhaps hiding behind their lack of understand of "well, that's middle school philosophy").

But let's not forget that growing up is a developmental process. We can do as much damage to the best and brightest with concepts too sophisticated for them as we can by boring them. Middle school kids have remarkable instincts, curiosity, and a love for learning. Making a twelve-year-old take calculus or read *Macbeth* is wonderful to brag about at grandma's but only a handful, not the masses, are capable. Those who are ready should not be held back. Those who aren't shouldn't be pushed too far or too fast. It's a tough balance. What parents deserve and should expect is honest communication and legitimate action, not idle promises, arbitrary course name changes, and "doing it like the high school."

("A bit defensive?" you ask. You bet!)

Middle school at risk? Absolutely - because there is no single right way or answer. It's not either-or. Some folks just don't get it! Self-concept and individualized attention AND hard work and achievement <u>can</u> be accomplished, simultaneously! But that's very hard and smart work.

2. Our instant-gratification therefore quick-fix society mentality.

We live in a society of remote control and 54 channels. We microwave a different meal for each member of the house. If something breaks, we buy new because it's cheaper than the repair. We've cured just about everything, or we just change the channel and pretend it doesn't exist. We have rules and laws and ordinances and signs to control our every action. We live in a quick fix society with a "what have you done for me today?"

mentality. We write rule upon rule upon law upon policy to prevent accidents. We have taken the word "accident" out of our vocabulary in order to affix blame and call the attorney to defend us or to attack.

Middle school at risk? "So, did my kid learn to read better — today? Prove it." "I want a new teacher and I don't care whether he's off team or not." "Why did the kids on the 'other team' get to go on a field trip?" "There's not enough hard work for the kids." "There's too much work for the kids." (and my personal favorite: "My kid doesn't lie.") "FIX IT NOW FOR MY KID."

Hey! They're twelve years old. Lighten up. Let them grow up. Let them experience a little failure. Let them learn to pick themselves up. Let them take some responsibility for their actions. Let them make a few mistakes. Let them develop instead of following a script.

Let's face it - junior high, with it's impersonal, one size fits all mentality, is a lot easier to keep everyone happy. You can blame everything on the rules and regulations.

AND, while I am on a roll, speaking of quick fixes, when will the beer and tobacco companies wake up and accept some responsibility?

Talk about hypocrisy! Let's sell beautiful, young, thin folks having a good time and convince youngsters that the only way they'll be able to climb mountains, get invited to parties, and be successful is to be beautiful ... and have a beer.

It would be great if that advertiser would spend a million dollars on "Be a mountain man - do your homework!" What we get instead are alcohol and tobacco advertising enticing our kids to think that perfection (beauty and adventure) is all that matters. I tire of the defense that "our ads are not targeted to teens." GIVE ME A BREAK.

AN OPEN LETTER TO THE FOLKS AT THE ALCOHOL AND TOBACCO COMPANIES:

YOUR ads are selling sex, popularity, excitement. So, let's figure this out (this is not rocket science). I want to be sexy, beautiful, adventuresome, and popular. You are telling me that that's what matters. So, since I do not look like, act like, or feel like those people in the ads, I need to do something with my body. Hmmmm, let's try diet pills. Maybe not eating. Maybe a drug. Maybe a beer. You want to sell beer on TV? Sell it. Spend millions on ads that say "buy our beer" - but STOP SELLING YOUR PERCEPTIONS OF PERFECTION TO OUR TEENAGERS.

Drink responsibly? HEY, ADVERTISE RESPONSIBLY!

Sincerely yours,

Jere Hochman
Jere Hochman

3. We've stolen the innocence from kids.

Michael Jackson - rock star accused of fondling a child.
Kurt Cobain - rock star suicide.
O.J. Simpson - football star accused of murder.
River Phoenix - actor overdose.
Darryl Strawberry - baseball star in rehab.

Video violence. Suicide. AIDS. Guns. Rape. Film at eleven? No. "Watch it live at five, right after the after–school special." "But kids, don't try this at home."

A few years ago our midwestern region had a year filled with dilemmas and tragedy. (And the media made sure they didn't miss one juicy detail.)

Several priests in the state next door were convicted of child molestation. Destructive floods hit the region. The media turned the saga of popular local television weatherman who committed suicide (allegedly) into a two-day soap opera. Acts of violence were committed in urban and suburban schools, only to be revisited in the media during sweeps months. And three months of paranoia and not being allowed to walk outside alone after the abduction/rape/murders of two thirteen year old girls were grossly and highly publicized, creating terror across the region. The media made sure that we didn't miss any of these.

As if the events weren't tragic enough, the daily bombardment from the media kept the fear at a frenzied level. As Arlo Guthrie noted in a recent concert, "there must be more money in showing bad news."

And, to top it all off, five hundred plus middle schoolers turned on the TV on a cold winter Sunday to see their brand new principal being arrested on allegations of child molestation after six months on the job. It was a heck of a year to be fourteen in our town! Middle school at risk? You bet.

Middle school kids aren't middle school kids anymore. They've seen it all but are told "don't touch." They can't and don't and shouldn't trust anyone. They're taking adult actions in an adult world with thirteen-year-old knowledge, maturity, and feelings. (PLEASE read that sentence again.)

Too many of their models are transparent, hypocritical, and sarcastic. It's easy to understand why a kid would be fearful of walking to school alone – going to school – or turning on the TV – in the 90's. Too many adults forget that the kids are thirteen. These are the same adults who wouldn't teach themselves or treat themselves the same way they teach and treat the thirteen-year-olds. Fortunately the schools are there to take care of kids – society isn't. But, hey, blame the schools anyway.

4. The Conservative Right, Parents of the 60s, & the Liberal But Probably Not Left.

My sixth grade teacher (in 1963) had a great line when she was advising me years later on how to approach my principal about teaching sex education:

Dear Mr. Principal and Parents: Your child is learning about sex. S/he learns it on the buses, in the locker room, in the bathrooms, and in the alleys on the way home from his/her classmates. Would you rather have your kid learn it there and from them – or in a classroom from me? Signed, Your Teacher.

So we've got a group of folks attempting to prohibit us from teaching anything meaningful. I actually had a parent tell me the schools shouldn't teach or be concerned with citizenship and responsibility. That's the parents' job. Our job is to teach math.

And, I suppose they believe that if they ban the right (wrong) (left) books, restrict their children's friends, and keep the schools from allowing the kids to question and think, they'll have complete control over them and protect them from the evils of society.

Surprise. Your kids are in for culture shock the day they go to college or when they first sneak out of the house.

Middle school at risk? We've stripped the schools of values and morals (not just teaching any but having or standing for any) and of teaching or reading anything that might cause kids to think, make their own judgments, or worse than that, be exposed to the realities of the world. Control in the elementary school is much simpler. By high school the course selections satisfy most as long as *Catcher in the Rye* isn't required. Middle school? Too touchy-feely. Banish it! Too controversial? Banish it. Too easy? Too hard?

Caught in the middle!

And, isn't it amazing, yes, in a democracy where all voices have the right to be heard, that one small group, one small uninformed group,

concerned about government control and monitoring of morals, has the power to grasp front page headlines and the valuable time and creativity of numerous administrators and teachers? And middle school, because it understands and respects the nature of the early adolescent, is ripe for the attack.

On the other hand, the bona fide sixties liberal parents don't trust government, school principals, or authority very much either. They don't get our innocuous rules to insure a little order. Their kids never lie and freedom of speech includes their child's freedom to wear a t-shirt bearing the wisdom of a male motorcyclist holding up a beer can in one hand and a chained naked female in the other. "My lawyer says he's got the right to wear it."

HEY - there's BEING RIGHT and there's DOING RIGHT. Just because you CAN do it doesn't mean you HAVE TO or SHOULD just to make a point. Take some responsibility, please.

The revolution was about rights and freedom, but they didn't have to teach algebra at Woodstock. A little personal responsibility is supposed to accompany the acquisition of those rights and freedom.

At-risk? Just like adolescence and adolescents, no one understands middle school. And if our mission and direction and methods are not clear and consistent, one of the many infamous "theys" out there will get us. Whew, democracy's tough!

on the anti—change critiques

Tell you what folks. You want heavy duty knowledge, competition among students, weeding out of students who don't make the cut, clear cut objectives (dare I use the term o-u-t-c-o-m-e-s?), no values or character development, just the right amount of technology blended with traditional knowledge development, scripted lessons so the teacher won't sneak in a little moral development, the right amount of humor, control over the teachable moment, and the perpetuation of capitalism as we know it? You want right and wrong answers and questions without the need to think?

Turn on "Jeopardy" or play "Trivial Pursuit."

Seriously. There is no script for life. You can protect your kids all you want, but some day they are going to take off and be out there all on their own. They're going to discover the artwork and novels of which they've been deprived. They're going to see some of those movies and even some of THOSE movies. They're going to be stuck in dozens of social situations because they've never been alone in social situations. They're going to go crazy with the freedom of time and choice on their college campus.

And, worst of all, they are going to resent those who kept them isolated from these few doses of reality, of decision-making, and of coping. No, worst of all is that when they need someone in a tough situation, whom do you think they'll call (or be afraid to call)?

And, while I am at it — outcomes based education (the real thing) simply states an outcome, like MEMORIZE the fifty states or the times tables. Then the kids are taught it. They do homework. They complain about that homework. They study. They take a test. Alone. They pass it. Or, they don't. So they study some more and take the test again. What's the big deal? It ain't (dear editor: I used "ain't" intentionally here) the best educational approach known to civilization, but it's not going to cause us to lose wars. (And personally, I don't see why anyone would use this method if he/she wants high cognitive learning.)

But the phrase has been taken out of context because the politicians (notice I didn't say educators) in a couple of states decided to use the method just to make sure more kids learned in their states and they slipped in a few affective objectives (The mistake buzzer should have gone off, but politicians try to fix everything). Since some are afraid the state is going to take over everything (or as I heard one speaker explain, the federal government will use this big computer – the contract is already complete – to store the results of all these tests including the attitudes of kids), it's the fault of the method, OBE. So now when someone considers painting the walls, changing the schedule, offering a new subject, or implementing some well-researched and thoughtful reform such as middle school principles, it gets labeled and creates a McCarthy–like scare. Hey, this is PUBLIC education – come on in and take a look.

Now it's school-to-work. And, as my critics know, I am the first to agree that I want neither state nor federal control over anything we do nor do I want to put kids in career paths. Do I believe that some corporate leaders would like the federal government to fix things, sort out kids, train kids to go into the world of work, and send the others to college? *Yes.* Do I think they are on target with their ideas and methods? *No.*

But that doesn't matter. What does matter is that every innovation, good idea, change, or concept that is not the way it was "when 'they' went to school" has NOTHING to do with OBE, school-to-work, or next year's federal initiative so PLEASE stop lumping it all together. There are a lot of schools doing things well (with room for improvement, of course) and this extreme criticism is killing it for everyone.

5. There are no final answers, no traditions, and most people have horrible memories of junior high.

That's right. This is same reason as why middle schools work. Most adults have horror stories about junior high. Either they or their classmate were publicly humiliated. Memorized poems forgotten. Wrong answers in math class. Being tardy in the big new school and chastised in front of the class. Wearing the wrong clothes. Wearing the right clothes after the in-group decided it was out. Too short. Too tall. Not in the smart group and feeling inadequate. In the smart group and outcast by the others. Sent to the office too much. Never set foot in the office. Girls made to feel inadequate. Boys, too. Too slow. Too weak. Too old. Too young. Too developed. Too underdeveloped. And the ultimate humiliations: 1) being called on when you don't know the answer, and 2) public showers. Some things haven't changed.

You have the horror story crowd who thinks middle school can't possibly be worthwhile, so the way we do it must be wrong. They think administrators/teachers/the school don't understand anything because *their* principals/teachers/school obviously didn't take care of them. They think the middle school teachers were demoted or inadequate high school teachers who either didn't care or weren't smart enough to teach high school. So, how can they be good enough for middle school?

At risk? There is no "known quantity" of middle school. Some adults have no memories of the principal or teacher encouraging them, no middle school traditions that were remembered at the twentieth reunion, and certainly no barometer of the right way or the way we always did it in junior high. At risk? Of course. It's always easy to retreat to the known and nostalgic.

6. 90's and 00's (What will we call that decade?) early adolescents, baby boomer parents, and baby boomer leaders.

No one understands adolescents. Happy one minute - pouting the next. You know the script. (See item #11.)

So, unhappy, complaining kids make for unhappy, complaining parents.

Now add the sixties and seventies in the formula.

When that 60s/70s parent was raised on a diet of "question authority," "never trust anyone over thirty," and "down with the establishment" AND their kid is unhappy, watch out! Time for change! They're on the phone and in your office within minutes (I, too, as a baby boomer daddy am guilty as charged.)

But, the kicker on this one is that those of us teaching and leading in the middle school *are* the same baby boomers. WE, too, grew up questioning authority, never trusting anyone over thirty, and fighting the establishment. And, guess who's the authority, over thirty, and the establishment? Us! So, not only do the parents enable, say "yes" to everything, and expect quick fixes, we also enable, compromise, and don't know the word "no."

In many cases, it's the teachers who question authority, don't trust anyone over thirty, and fight the establishment. Just because.

The result? We want to make everyone happy. We're suckers for a good self-esteem sob story. And since we never bought into that anti-materialism of the sixties, budgets mean little to us, not because we dismiss 'things,' but because we don't understand 'no' or budgets.

So, the equation we've developed is a group of kids who test (and need) limits and a group of adults who don't know how to say no or set limits (and even celebrate coloring outside the lines). It's like pouring gas on a raging fire (or hormones).

The result? Ambiguity. Lack of structure. Too much creativity and flexibility and not enough order, discipline, and homework. Too much "either" or too much "or" but not a blend of anything. Inconsistency. Lack of definition. And that puts us at risk!

From a culture and organizational perspective, we went from the industrial comply-just-because school of the fifties to the "if it feels good do it" school of the seventies and never learned the value of systems, process, and wholeness. So instead of doing whole language, many teachers did the other half. Bath water got thrown out with babies. A little balance would be nice.

Middle school at-risk? Once again, because of the "unknown quantity" of who and why we are - and because there will never be enough structure for some and too much for others, because parents will put their kid and their unique request ahead of what's best for the group or because the authority has reasons for things being that way, we're at risk of losing our philosophy and our stance on what we believe and know.

7. Oldest children.

You can always tell which parents have their oldest child in the middle school. They're uptight. They're intense. They don't understand why their kid is saying no, not doing his/her homework, not consuming books, or not dressing neatly. "Oh, honey, it must be the school's fault."

"In fifth grade my child turned in the neatest papers, her room was always clean, she read extra books for extra-credit book reports, and she never stood in front of the mirror making faces and saying curse words. She didn't spend hours on the phone or hours crying because no one called. She played with dolls (or he traded baseball cards). What happened?"

And of course, it's the school's fault because that's the only thing that's changed. (See item #11 - and please, printipals teach parents about adolescents, hormones, growth, development, and puberty.)

By the time their oldest children are in ninth grade, these same parents are seasoned and giving sage advice to other parents. But for those intervening three years, we at school bite our tongues waiting for the kids to grow up and the parents to understand.

At risk? Annually, of losing the ground we've gained. Fortunately there are parents of second and third kids in the school, and they will speak out and say, "my kid survived - they have to grow through it."

8. The hurried child get-my-kid-in-Harvard we're-way-behind-Japan syndrome.

Forget anything that smacks of process, inquiry, social value, or giving kids room to grow. Track my kid. Push my kid. Assign more. I did drill and practice and I turned out all right. No group work. Don't put him with "those" kids, or "those" kids, or even "those" kids. Why is my kid doing a poster? He could be writing a dissertation. (Of course, if the poster or project or hands-on activity IS mindless collage-making in lieu of thinking about and presenting something with purpose, we deserve every bit of criticism we get.)

The kids write daily; produce research and report on it routinely; dig into primary and secondary sources to develop their own hypotheses and studies and what do we hear about? The collage the kid did instead of a book report.

As for the foreign competition. Pardon me. Are you willing to allow schools to determine when your child is only thirteen what his/her future will be? Or would you prefer your child have a chance to excel, be a late bloomer, or perhaps even decide for herself?

9. Professionals who aren't.

How do you know a middle school is at-risk? When one discovers teachers who think professionalism means "what have you done for me today?" and believe that one should count hours, minutes, numbers of committees, numbers of preps, and numbers of kids. Think about it.

10. Tampering with systems, the boiled frog syndrome, "does it fit," and "so what?"

The ends of middle school, of schooling of any age child or adult, should be the principles which motivate and drive us. Kids need structure. Kids need to explore. Kids need to be challenged and stretched academically. Fine. Routine exploratory blocks which includes technology, integrated arts, and studies of culture will achieve that end. They are not ends in themselves. If they were, we'd still be using slide rules, drill presses, and ditto machines.

But, as noted above and reiterated (and reverberated) later, we have institutionalized our innovations. The "new" middle school is now the "tradition." We have tampered with systems and concepts and ideas. Fine tuning is necessary. Replacing programs within systems is necessary. Two concerns, however, exist.

1) Tampering: Do those making the changes have knowledge of the original rationale for the system or program? Making a big school seem small to a twelve year old may have been the biggest priority when designing the school. Change a few leaders and pretty soon the school is back to a junior high day with bells ringing everywhere, and the whole school crowded in the hall eight times a day.

There's nothing wrong with "messing with success" but we need to remember the success is NOT in *what* we do. The success is in the *why* we do it.

2) Complacency: "We've always done it that way." "We did it that way when s/he was here. Why should we change it?" "No, I can't remember why we did it that way but that's just the way it is." "Why should we

consider changing that? If it ain't broke, don't fix it."
Well, you know the story of the boiled frog. Put the frog in a vat of boiling water. It reacts and jumps out as fast as it can. Put a frog in a vat of cold water and slowly increase the heat to a boil. The frog dies in the water.

We had better take a very close look at our middle schools and make sure that we aren't using the "it's against middle philosophy" as a cop-out response – that we haven't turned our innovations and organizational *means* into *ends* – that we clearly understand purpose – that we continue to ask "why?" often.

11. "What did you guys do to my kid?"

Oh, you can figure this one out. Most adults don't get (nor remember — nor want to remember — nor want to face up to) puberty. So, their kid turns eleven and goes just a little bit off the wall, and ...

You know the lines. Mood swings. On a cloud one minute, pouting the next. In their own world. Never met a mirror

they didn't like. (Aren't you a little tired of all the "let's make fun of the middle schooler" descriptions?) But regardless of the description, the actions that cause them are real and no one quite understands them.

As one seventh grade dad said to me one afternoon, "What did you guys do to my kid?"

"Let's see," says another parent. "I haven't changed. We didn't move. We eat about the same meals we've always eaten. No significant changes in weather patterns. Same water. What's different? WHAT'S DIFFERENT! It must be the school - that middle school (or in this case junior high, doesn't really matter). That's it - it's the school's fault!"

And as long as kids go through puberty, middle schools will be at-risk. You have to blame somebody!

(But there's also the chance that someone will say the school IS successful, and that brings us to the topic of culture.)

CHAPTER 5   It's All Culture

Culture.

Culture?

Yes, culture!

(Please don't let the word scare you –
just substitute "the way
things are around here"
and think about your
classroom or school.)

"Plastics."

Remember the famous line from the 60s revealing the expected key to Dustin Hoffman's future?

I suppose if someone were going to remake *The Graduate,* perhaps an educational version, the not-so-distinguished know-it-all at the cocktail party would walk up to a naive Tom Cruise (instead of Dustin) playing the role of Benjamin Braddock and whisper one word: (choose one from the list below).

"Benjamin, I only have one thing to say to you: TQM, chaos theory, quality, portfolios, teaming, accelerated school, computer-assisted instruction, authentic assessment, coopera-collabor-asserti-win/win-nonviol-conflictresolutive discipline, or some other hot topic."

Plastics. Technology. Innovation. Standards. The "saviors of education" (and society) come and go. What matters is what we do with them. What matters is how we use them, implement them, and think about them.

What is the hidden meaning behind the selected phrase that will change our future and the actions it symbolizes? Culture.

Culture, more often than not, gets the rap for all problems and successes. "Oh, it's just the culture." "The new principal? Oh, she doesn't understand the culture, yet!" "If you're going to fit in here, you need to understand the culture."

Well, that may all be true but two vital points must be addressed in this discussion of success, of "making 'it' happen" in middle school.

First, we all know that the right answer is the teacher in the classroom.

Second, leaders have a responsibility to lead excellent teachers and schools to grow, not manage them. It is the leader who frames that culture. The program doesn't matter. It's what one does with it.

The challenge? It's the vision thing and the synergy thing. It's the culture. Imagine every classroom a haven for achievement, engagement, and belonging (kids and adults). Tie them together with a thread of "middle school philosophy" (whatever that means) and you've got a successful middle school filled with motivation and productivity, a school filled with meaningful work and working at means, and a school that is making "it" happen. Great teachers and leadership. That's all "it" takes (or needs). And the elusive "it" - that's the culture!

Think about it.
(That's right - get out your pencil and use the space below.)

Think about a few schools you have visited. Think about the school where you teach (everyone is a teacher no matter what their position) now, the school you attended, the schools you have visited, or maybe your kid's school. Jot down a few things they have in common. Homework? Texts? Tests? Teams? Homerooms?

Conferences? It doesn't have to be anything terribly unique or dramatic.

Now ask yourself, "Self, how do these schools view/see this topic? How does each 'do' teaming? How does each 'do' conferences?"

Observations? Same topic but different interpretations. It's not the "what" they are doing but rather the "why? and the "how?" and the meaning it infers. and THAT is the culture.

"It's the culture"

How often have we heard it?
"The new guy just doesn't seem to fit in."
It's the culture.

"You certainly take a lot of field trips."
It's the culture.

"I don't understand why we do it this way.
No other district does it that way."
It's the culture.

"May I be honest about something?
I have never seen so much
involvement of parents from all races."
It's the culture.

"Every teacher in the school
emphasizes organizational skills."
It's the culture.

"This place seems to manage by
anticipating the worst—case scenario."
It's the culture.

Your examples?

It's the culture.

If culture is the answer to everything, then perhaps it's time to ask what it is.

What's culture?

and then...
instead of asking what program we want, we'll ask, "what kind of culture do we want?"

The term culture, originating from its most general perspective as applied to groups or societies; their respective knowledge, rules, and beliefs; and the relationship among the individuals in each setting, is founded in research from several disciplines. Though most prevalent in anthropology, research and application of "culture" is founded in cognitive psychology, education, sociology, organizational analyses, and others.

Perhaps it is the general application of the term and prescribed research-specific definitions that causes vagueness and generality in using the term, consequently prohibiting a specific across-the-research agreed upon application and definition. It's a lot like defining "life!"

Culture, without all the research jargon?
It's the way we do things around here; and the *why* we do things around here, too. In some cases it's the "way we have always done things around here" but those folks have usually forgotten the why. Others may think of it as the "way we envision doing things around here."

No matter how you define it, analyze it, or think about it, it's all culture, it's just the way things are. Of significance is how we read it, how we describe it, and then what we do after we've started that process.

Perhaps this vagueness has kept researchers from applying the term when determining successful schooling. Too elusive. Too vague. And, too "touch-feely." (Could our instant gratification, what-have-you-done-for-me-today society tolerate such obscure non-measures?) Consequently, educators have resorted to check-list, countable, quantifiable, observable, and measurable standards to determine school success.

Culture: "Well, it feels right."

It's a lot like spelling and grammar. It either sounds right and looks right - or it doesn't.

Culture in the classroom, in the school? It either sounds right and looks right and feels right, or it doesn't.

The way I see it, a metaphor of a successful school is a fluid poem, a passionate editorial, or a powerful speech, not a well- edited, grammatically correct instruction manual or legal brief. Both could be cited as "well written" but their literary "cultures" are quite different. And, I liken working with kids much more to writing poetry than a policy statement.

Culture: Three perspectives on "how we measure and describe success around here?"

(The three categories introduced below, technical, illusory, and constructive, are based on the work of Popkewitz, Tabachnik, and Wehlage in their study, *The Myth of Educational Reform.* More on that later but they deserve the credit - I have just borrowed it to look at middle school.)

One observer may quantify programs to intervene for at-risk students, accuracy of procedures followed in handling discipline offenses, and percentile improvements in standardized test scores and declare the school a success, albeit technical.

Perceived success in this school? "More is better" (or less - it depends what you're measuring).

Observations on this style of success? If you can count it, it shouldn't count (kids, test scores, participants, awards).

(hint: technical culture)

Another observer may be impressed with the presence of honor rolls, 100% faculty participation in contributions to local charities, insignificant additions of one day to a school year to declare increased excellence, required student volunteering (oxymoron alert), and ongoing celebrations of _____ Day, or "of the year" award and declare the school a success, albeit illusory.

Perceived success in this school? "Looks pretty good from here."

Observations on this style of success? To quote the ill fated campaign of Walter Mondale - "Where's the beef?"

(hint: illusory culture)

Yet another observer, however, may acquire the skills and courage to assess the school and recognize the integration of practices, systems, and principles and cite successes based on meaningful work and professionalism.

Perceived success in this school? Well, it sort of feels right. No, seriously. Success? What are folks actually doing? Is it meaningful? Productive? Are words like *authentic, substantive, useful, applicable,* and *principled* used as adjectives to describe the activity and products in the school?

(hint: constructive culture)

Culture:

"One man's ceiling
is another man's floor"

"Partly Sunny!" or "Partly Cloudy"

"You say tomAto, I say tomAHto."
(or Reading Culture)

Like the umpire in baseball who declares "it ain't a strike until I call it," the observer of school organization determines success assessing the culture (even if they don't know it by that term).

So, observe and assess: What's your "read" on these and the others, below?

Mrs. Z. stands at the doorway greeting the kids as they enter. *Get that homework done last night, Carlos? Good for you. Jack, you cleaned out your notebook, all right! Becky, (whispering) remember, I won't call on you unless you raise your hand today, just like we agreed.*

Okay, everyone – daily language lab books out. Talk to your neighbor – tell him or her about the last time you heard someone really happy about or excited about something. (noise) Now, write one or two sentences about it. (pause). Now, add one sentence with something someone else said – and add some emphasis to it. Remember those quotation marks in the right place. (pause) Okay, reread yours to yourself. (pause) Now trade notebooks with someone – make a suggestion for one addition, one deletion, and one change. (pause) Okay, before you edit your own, let's hear from someone who, no, wait, everyone get ready to read your own out loud – and read it with a lot of inflection when you get to those quotes. Ready? Go. (noise) Good, now those of you whom I heard shouting your sentences, what should I expect to see at the end of the sentence?

(Becky's hand flies up). *An exclamation point!*

OBSERVER A on Mrs. Z's lesson:
___+___ Anticipatory Set
___−___ Statement of objective
___−___ Guided practice

Mrs. Z, it took some time to get your class started. The delays at the doorway may have been beneficial for those to whom you spoke but the rest of the class was roaming the room waiting for the class to begin. The pace of this opening section was good but there was much too much noise for students to focus on their daily language. What was the objective of the lesson? Why didn't you use the lesson from the Daily Language series of "sentences to edit at the start of class"? How will you know how Becky is doing if you only call on her when she knows the answer?

OBSERVER B on Mrs. Z's lesson:

_____ Anticipatory Set

_____ Statement of objective

_____ Guided practice

Mrs. Z. Great class beginning. You hooked kids with the "what you saw at home or on TV" - I am sure they concentrated more on sentences as a result of that bit of relevance. Reading aloud with inflection certainly emphasized your lesson on quotations and exclamatory punctuation. I especially like the way you handled Becky. Did you see her participation? 100% just knowing she wasn't going to be put on the spot. Level of concern was just right.

_____

So what?

(folks interested in success ask "so what?" a lot).

As noted, it's all culture. Placing a value on it, positive or negative, healthy or ill, democratic or autocratic, businesslike, loosely-coupled, flexible, energetic or other descriptors rests in the perceptions of the observer and what s/he brings to the party. "One man's ceiling is another man's floor."

I have walked into hundreds of classrooms and know that what I see and what another observer sees are two very different things. As illustrated in the example, two observers, same classroom, two very different perceptions. That's where the culture enters the picture.

Culture of the School

The study by Popkewitz, Tabachnick, and Wehlage (1982) may be the key to understanding culture and school success. Their study of "exemplary" Individually Guided Education (IGE) schools and the "myth of educational reform" is essentially a treatise on school cultures cited as *technical, illusory,* and *constructive.* As concepts of culture exemplified by the practices at each of the schools, the authors explore attributes of each in terms of work, knowledge, and professionalism citing the value of such attributes in considering features of authority, legitimacy, and social control in the routine of the school.

:-{ Whoa. Wait a minute. This sounds like part of a doctoral dissertation. So, noooowww it makes sense. This is one of those "turn the dissertation into a book" deals, and I am expected to make it apply to my school or my classroom.

Well, uh, ... YES.

However...

(of course, there's a 'however' whenever one tries to rationalize and I told you, I can rationalize anything that makes sense for teaching kids)

it does apply. It's about kids. It's about what adults do. It's about culture. You know, if it looks like a duck, walks like a duck, floats like a duck, and quacks like a duck, well, it's probably a duck. If we are going to explore successful schooling, let's look at schools

(not at businesses or at "the way we did it when I was growing up").

Culture comes in all kinds of packages.

And, to revise the question posed earlier: could your classroom or school be found guilty by a jury of your peers for maintaining the culture of a successful school?

What evidence would you bring to the trial? Test scores? Happy kids? Empowered parents? An advisory program? Invigorated teachers? Decisions made by those teachers in planning? Decisions made by those teachers on their feet? (Some-one once told me that "one on his/her feet is better than two in their seats" - now *that's* reading the culture of the classroom.)

Anyway, here comes the research part.

ASIDE: The way I see it, you can either skip this part and get to the "how to" part (be warned, however, that those who do read this section will have you pegged "technical/illusory" in about three pages) or you can face the theoretical music and read on. (To carry out the metaphor, you'll not only be able to face the music, you'll be able to conduct the orchestra as your colleagues and you construct new tunes, themes, story lines as part of your daily work.) Of course, if you teach/lead by instinct and it works, well, this is all just more for you to run through your lens anyway.

Schooling – in terms of professional culture

Upon reflection of their observations and research in dozens of Individually Guided Education (IGE) schools, Popkewitz, Tabachnik, and Wehlage recognized that these schools which were to be quite similar in their curriculum, instruction, and modes of operation were quite different. The authors' recognition of that which makes schools different is the basis of their book, titled appropriately, *The Myth of Educational Reform*. The title alone leads one's thoughts through a network of professional experiences and reactions to current issues and their current status. The logic begins with the proposition that a school is a social institution, an organization for work, and a home for knowledge. Consider the stuff of schools as purported by the authors.

Schools are places of work where students and teachers interact to alter and improve their world, establish social relations, and realize human purpose. Schools are also places where conceptions of knowledge are distributed and maintained; implicit in this discourse are ways of reasoning and communicating about social relations, social conditions, and social authority. Finally, schools are staffed by an occupational group whose activities give legitimacy to patterns of work and conceptions of knowledge. Often that group uses the label "professional" to establish its status, privileges, and control. (p. 11)

When reflecting upon restructuring, successful schooling, or the status quo, the authors' categories of knowledge, work, and authority are most appropriate and simplistically, all inclusive. If "it's all culture" and we are to interpret the culture of the school, these categories work well for us.

School?

Knowledge.

Work.

Authority.

In an analysis of the culture of authority in schools, Elmore (1987) refers to culture as the "normative order" within which teachers and students learn in schools. Elmore explains culture's "role" as "defining and legitimating inequality" and defining this process as "authority."

Citing essential cultural elements translated to "schooling," Bates (1981) explains that culture gives meaning to life in terms of beliefs, languages, rituals, knowledge, conventions, courtesies, and artifacts, in short, the cultural baggage of any group are the resources from which individual and social identity are constructed. They provide the framework upon which the individual constructs his understanding of the world and of himself. Part of this baggage is factual. It is empirical, descriptive, objective. Another part of this cultural baggage, perhaps the greater part, is mythical. It is concerned not with facts but with meaning: that is, with the interpretative and prescriptive rules which provide the basis for understanding and action. (p. 108)

Sergiovanni (1987) explains the potential administrative link to culture noting that "cultural life in schools is constructed reality, and school principals can play a key role in building this reality" (p. 59). Concurrently, the author cites Bates' explanation that the culture is a "product of conflict and negotiation over definitions and situations" and that "the administrative influence on school language, metaphor, myths, and rituals is a major factor in the determination of the culture which is reproduced in the consciousness of teacher and pupils" (p. 59).

Okay, this is all pretty heavy for what up until now has been an "in your face" approach to discussing middle school. The theory is critical. Sure, it validates a little of what I have said and gives me a little credence, but its value goes well beyond that.

We get tested all the time. It's easy to spout off tirades about culture or believing in the kids or democracy until the first crisis or critic surfaces. Open House speeches and job interviews always glow, but the proverbial rubber hits the road when the parent marches into your office or the Board marches you into its meeting. Are you still talking about equity and level playing fields? How long do you hold out before you cave in to pull-out gifted programs or pulling kids off team to schedule orchestra? Do you still do your government simulation when the standardized test scores on government standards dropped?

You see, it's all culture. It's all the $1.00 words above linked with your instincts and the values and skill you possess.

And, I argue that it is the cognition of the leader - the teacher, the principal, the team leader - that is the key to determining culture! (Remember the part about reading culture and planning schooling simultaneously?)

Essentially, the way we define our work, our professional relationships, and our learned and constructed knowledge (and "we" are the adults and kids) is culture.

Essentially, culture is a cognitive structure embedded in leaders.

Essentially, leaders are the adults in every classroom and every school office.

Whew! Perhaps this is a good time to stop, to think, to write, and to read or watch something light!

CHAPTER 6 Culture: The Litmus Test of Successful (Middle) Schooling

As we proceed to think about the middle school, consider more specifically that which makes it a success or not.

Is success...

- *found in practices of interdisciplinary units, teaming, research-based instruction, exploratory blocks, and advisory programs?*
- *found in the programs with their respective rationale for organizational skills, reading across the disciplines, heterogeneous grouping, academic intervention plans, mentoring programs, relationships with universities, parent volunteer programs, and homebase periods?*
- *found in the school's dedication to principles of authentic achievement, academic engagement, school membership, substantive conversation, equity, and other principles of democracy?*

Or, is success

- *embedded in a particular integration of all three "levels" of success characteristics?*

     (Think about it. Of course it is, or I wouldn't have offered that proposition.)

(Yes, I know we've gotten a long way from teaming and advisory and exploratory blocks, but if you/we are serious about this, it's time we stopped being satisfied with "Of course we're a successful middle school because we've got teaming" and get serious about successful schooling).

Well,

ASSUMING that we are seeking a "successful" school

(and we know that success is embedded in great teaching, happy kids, solid achievement, a sense of belongingness, just the right amount of academic rigor, kids not being put down, and a variety of other isolated yet significant attributes), and

ASSUMING that "it's all culture," which is a subjective perspective based on who is conceiving or who is perceiving the organization and its culture, respectively, and

ASSUMING that middle schools are based on several key propositions about kids and teaching and organization; on the establishment of well designed systems to achieve those ends; and on the innovative, dynamic, hands on, experiential, structured daily practices ...

it is time to figure out how to describe it and how to get there!

If you have been following the logic of this network of thought, three things should be clear:

First, success is found in the most simple, common sense, "of course," "ah ha" actions of our daily work as well as in the most complex cognitive connections (alliteration aside) between beliefs and systems and practices.

Second, success is found in systems and patterns and connections and in the bridges between the practices (and even programs) and the principles of middle school.

Third, success is found in the culture. If it's all culture, then the middle school anthropologist must look at the culture through a different lens, with a unique mind set, and look at the whole package, and not just what's on the surface.

So What?

The examination of middle school practices, concepts, and beliefs illustrates that in efficient schools, practices, concepts, and beliefs can exist in isolation. Each translates to a program or component of the school with a linear means-ends value. In these schools, technical or illusory cultures prevail with very little substance beyond quantitative results or no-substance events.

The constructivist school defined throughout, on the other hand, integrates thoughts about kids and middle school. It is the connection between beliefs, systems, and practice. And, it's a little common sense.

DID YOU CATCH THAT?

The answer to successful culture is the combination of

1) BELIEFS ABOUT KIDS, PROFESSIONALS, AND LEARNING, AND

2) CONSISTENCY AND FLUIDITY IN PRINCIPLES, PATTERNS (SYSTEMS), AND PRACTICES.

Practices are always viewed as means, not ends, and professionals recognize that there is always more to learn and incorporate. Concepts are framed as systems of the school, connected to other systems as well as to practices and beliefs. Principles upon which the school is based are observable throughout the practices and systems. Participants in the school recognize that the playing field and its parameters have been established, but that each game is different. And it is all founded on what we know and think and feel and believe about kids, professionals, and genuine learning.

Thinking About Culture, or "It ain't a strike until I call it"

B: "It's not fair. We pay for those snacks. How can they just decide to not sell them."

L: "Didn't you hear what he said? From now on you can only purchase one snack with lunch. Big deal. It's all lard and sugar anyway."

D: "That's all I eat. So I'm supposed to eat those plate lunches now."

Q: "Hey, I don't *have* a choice so watch what you're saying. The point is that no one asked us. They sell those things to make up for what they lose on the nutritious stuff. That means we're paying more than we should - probably a 60% mark up. So, they don't sell more, the price goes up, and, they never asked us."

R: "Yeah, that's what's like buggin' me. They didn't even ask."

J: "I think it's just a power thing. They're trying to show who's the boss. Those teachers meet every Thursday morning and decide everything. No one ever asks us. I mean, like, well, if they want us to cut down on eating that crap, oops, sorry Mrs. V., eating that junk, just tell us. We'll cut back."

R: "Well, like I heard some parents called and complained to the main office about the junk food. That's why they changed it."

N: "Let's boycott. If no one buys the desserts and snacks that'll show em."

W: "Did you forget, that's what they want! But, if everyone brings their lunch, they'll go broke!"

Scenarios and Conversations to Help Us Think About Culture

A: "Let's sit in — nobody leave the cafeteria today."

B: "Let's hang posters demanding what we want."

D: "Well, I am your student council representative, why don't you give us a chance to work on it first?"

Ms V: "Okay, hold it — quick — notebooks out — everyone — writing — first, what are your thoughts about this issue? Be honest, and if you could care less, explain that, too. Second, how should you proceed?

Ms V: "Everyone — second part, how should we proceed? Find the verb and touch it — I am calling on everyone!

        Al? Good, 'I think we should boycott' — what's the verb? Good. Dale? 'drop it'. Debbie? 'Delegate it to the student council rep,' correct? Beth? 'Hang posters' — okay. Any one else?

        Have we ever talked about Luther and the 95 Theses? I know the Declaration of Independence is on your brains. Does 'taxation without representation' ring a bell? Remember we read the *Letter from A Birmingham Jail*? Do you remember that approach?"

All: "Civil disobedience."

Ms V: "Good. Now, do you remember the approach? Did the group just start a boycott? Did the colonists just start tossing tea into the harbor? Or did they try other means first?"

N: "Well I think we should ..."

YOU MAKE THE CALL

CLASSROOM OBSERVATION

TEACHER: Ms V.
OBSERVER: YOU!

DATE: _____
CLASS: Morning LANG/SS

Comments:

_____

_____

_____

_____

_____

CLASSROOM OBSERVATION

TEACHER: <u>Ms V.</u>   DATE: _____
OBSERVER: Mr. T.

CLASS: <u>Morning LANG/SS</u>

Comments:

Ms V., I was intrigued by the way you handled Bill's original question. It is important to allow student's to express their feelings and opinions, especially in social studies. However, by allowing the conversation to go on so long, some very touchy subjects were raised, and you may have encouraged the students to carry out a plan of protest. Quentin's comment about his free lunch was inappropriate. What book did you hand him after class? Perhaps, too, you can help me understand why you would bring up Martin Luther and religion in social studies. This is public school. In the future I suggest you not allow such discussions to go on so long. Furthermore, I would prefer that you begin your class with D.O.L (daily oral language) as do the rest of the seventh grade teachers. Your mural on "Celebrate Diversity" looks very good. Please be sure the blinds in your room are at mid level, as you have a window that faces the front of the school.

CLASSROOM OBSERVATION

TEACHER: <u>Ms V.</u>   DATE: _____
OBSERVER: Mrs. K.

CLASS: <u>Morning LANG/SS</u>

Comments

Rita, what a dynamic lesson! The rapport that you have established between you and your kids and among your kids is exemplary. It appears that your room is a "risk free" environment where students are confident to reveal who they are and where they can question you, each other, and, as the bumper sticker says, "question authority" without the fear of put down. Asking students to compare their daily lives to situations in history is the stuff of "relevance." I could see how motivated they were to follow the discussion and perhaps to act on their concerns. I appreciate your dissuading the kids from leaping into protest for the sake of protest. Can you think of some ways they might get to see what was happening? Perhaps assigning roles of observer, reporter, and others will embellish the activities for those not as concerned about the issue of the day. I liked the way you had each student 'touch the verb' and others like that through-out the lesson. You got the distracted kids back on task, made up for the language routine that was missed, and kept the discussion focused. Good lesson! I am eager to drop in again soon.

Scenario B
Model for Teaming

Definition: Teaming is a means of assigning approximately 100 students to a team of four teachers for the equivalent of five periods a day in one geographic location, accessible to other resources, human and material.

Principles:

- Big schools need to feel smaller for students and adults.

- Students need to develop trust and academic relationships among their peers in order to take risks in study.

- Teachers and students need a "homebase" within the school.

- Block of time scheduling allows for grouping and regrouping; flexible scheduling; better use of time; and fewer trips down the halls.

- Skills in organization, study, research, reporting, writing, measurement, analyzing data, and others are used in all subjects and should be reinforced throughout the day and units.

- Some topics of study are not "discipline" or "subject" specific.

- Allowing teachers to be "in control" of a group of students, of space, the calendar, and time is desirable.

Conversations with Mr. T., a principal

Mr. R: Mr. T., You know that I am coaching wrestling over at the high school this year. Any chance I can leave at 2:50, it's just our team planning period anyway?

Mr. T: Sure, no problem, if the team questions, tell them to see me.

***

Mrs. L: Adam, you know that you've scheduled seven kids off team for three periods?

Mr. T: Yes, I know. Three of them are in orchestra and we couldn't schedule them any other way. The other four, well, their parents called and they all wanted their kids to have Mr. R on the other team for science.

Mrs. L: Do you realize the impact seven kids off team has on our scheduling double periods, field trips, even basic assignments? Adam, how could you do this?

Mr. T: I have my priorities, Mrs. L.

***

Mrs. G: Mr. T., we've estimated it's going to take us about a half day and about $75 in hardware to move those twenty lockers from the seventh grade floor to the eighth. Is there any way those twenty eighth graders could just go down to the seventh grade floor to get to their lockers instead of moving them?

Mr. T: Good suggestion. Yes, sure, leave them where they are.

***

Dr. O: Adam, I just wanted to let you know, you might get a few calls. We're going to regroup the kids for the next six week block. Hmmm? That means we'll be mixing the Algebra and General Algebra kids. They're both on the chapter on binomials, so it's not that much of a problem. We're starting our unit on immigration, so they'll all be doing demographics research and applying the formulae anyway.

Mr. T: Well, Dr. O, I suggest you look at your scheduling and come up with another way to do that. How will it look when I have to face those accelerated algebra kids' parents and tell them we're not grouping them separately? And, I have to tell you, I am a little leery of 'demographics' research. What exactly does that mean?

Conversations with Mrs. K., also a principal

Mr. R: Mrs. K., You know that I am coaching wrestling over at the high school this year. Any chance I can leave at 2:50, it's just our team planning period anyway?

Mrs. K: "Just your teaming period?" Sorry Steve, that won't work. The team meeting is critical to everything we do. Imagine your doctor not showing up for consultation before your surgery? Imagine you and your football assistants over at the high school not scouting and not meeting before a game.

***

Mrs. L: Jane, do you know that you've scheduled seven kids off team for three periods?

Mrs. K: Seven? Three of them are in orchestra and we couldn't schedule

them any other way but who are the other four? I had some parents call to assign their kids to a specific teacher but they shouldn't have been scheduled. Let me see what happened.

Mrs. L: And the orchestra?

Mrs. K: I'm sorry Ellen. We're a year away from being able to send those kids to both teams but I talked to Alyn about it. She said that when either of you reschedules she'll work with you with some independent rehearsals, but you'll need to understand a "no" around concerts.

***

Mrs. G: Mrs. K., we've estimated it's going to take us about a half day and about $75 in hardware to move those twenty lockers from the seventh grade floor to the eighth. Is there any way those twenty eighth graders could just go down those steps to get to their lockers instead of moving them?

Mrs. K: They have to be moved. If you need help, let me know.

***

Dr. O: Jane, just wanted to let you know, you might get a few calls. We're going to regroup the kids for the next six week block. Hmmm? That means we'll be mixing the Algebra and General Algebra kids. They're both on the chapter on binomials so it's not that much of a problem. We're starting our unit on immigration so they'll all be doing demographics research and applying the formulae anyway.

Mr. T: Thanks for the warning but that's why we block and team the kids in the first place. I'll be interested in what happens to the level of performance of the general kids when we mix everyone together. Aim high — I bet they jump right in.

Constructing Meaning of Scenarios:
The Concepts of Technical, Illusory, and Constructivist Cultures

Scenario A illustrates that in the same setting, program, or school, in the same "culture," two observers will see the same thing but attribute two very different meanings. Similarly, as noted in Scenario B and the study that follows, two different organizations and their respective leaders will implement the same system, even based on the same set of beliefs, and yet end up with two very different programs. That is where the singular observer (and eventually the leadership) comes in and it is the basis of our discovery of the successful middle school.

We can all rattle off the elements of the "good" middle school. Teaming, advisory, block scheduling, interdisciplinary units and so on. But three schools implementing teaming, advisory, block scheduling, interdisciplinary units and so on will prove to be quite different. That is what

Popkewitz, Tabachnik, and Wehlage discovered in their study of schools implementing Individually Guided Education.

Remember back in Chapter Five it was established that schools are places of work and that schools should be contemplated in terms of professionalism, authority, relationships, concepts of knowledge, and work.

That in itself is a revolutionary concept the quick fix world of innovation and a "whad'ya'get" mentality. Of significance at this juncture is the notion that words like *work*, *authority*, *relationships*, and *knowledge* have no value without adjectives, without attributes or exemplars. *Relationships?* Positive relationships? Healthy relationships? Interpersonal relationships? Professional relationships?

What is "quality work" anyway? Meaningful work? Authentic assessment?

Authority can be autocratic, democratic, or laissez-faire. Knowledge can be rote, discovered, memorized, factual, mythical, or trivial. Knowing that schools are culture and that "it's all culture" only provides a new lens through which we can look at schools.

The adjectives are critical! The adjectives distinguish the attributes of the culture and assist us in exploring the roots of success, the type of culture. A brief look at the schools discussed in *The Myth of Educational Reform* provides a beneficial framework for us to continue.

Technical schooling

Popkewitz and associates cite elements of technical schooling as:

1) a curriculum development process dominated by the assumptions of rational planning, and resulting in a professional search for efficiency which emphasizes intellectual certainty and standardization; 2) the organization of classroom discourse, schoolwork, and social interaction in such a way as to sustain and legitimize routines and technical procedures; 3) the creation of a warm, supportive psychological environment that makes it pleasant for pupils to participate in the routines of school life; 4) the assignment of peripheral status to ambiguity, creativity, and nonstandardized learning, which are not institutionally sanctioned even when they are personally valued by teachers; and 5) professional and community support of standardization and efficiency as normal and reasonable values in the conduct of schooling.

— pp. 61-62

Constructive schooling

In contrast, the institutional character of the "constructive" Kennedy school reveals differences in terms of conditions of meaningful work and concepts of "produced" knowledge. At Kennedy, constructive schooling:

involves problematic thinking, aesthetic expression, and the integration of skills and knowledge in complex activities. This takes place in an atmosphere in which schoolwork is playful and active, and in which an ambiguous concept of knowledge emerges. A range of options in subject matter and method of presentation is available to teachers. Greater reliance is placed upon shared, cooperative educational tasks in which children have increased discretion.

— p. 107

Illusory schooling

The authors' description of "illusory" schooling varies greatly from the achievement founded in the technical and constructive school and an internal contradiction between content and display of acquired knowledge and between practice and motivation. Describing illusory schools, the authors explain:

There were facts and subjects to be taught, but the rituals and ceremonies of the formal curriculum were unrelated to this content and therefore could not produce success for most pupils. The social processes of the daily activities, however, did have substantive meaning. Teachers perceived the failure to learn as a result of conditions in the children's lives (broken home, indifference to academic values, lack of educational readiness), which were believed to make achievement impossible for all but a lucky few. The shortcomings of the schools were attributed to the inadequacies of the poor and minority communities in which the schools were situated.

The label 'illusory' applies to both the images and the details of life in these schools - the false impressions created by everyday patterns of activity, and the substantive values represented by these patterns of schooling. The emphasis on community pathology, pedagogy as therapy, and ritual gives these schools meaning different from those of the technical and constructive schools.

— pp. 121-122

The significance of these categories? Take a look at two more.

Issue: Discipline

PHONE RINGS... The boys did what? Shaving cream on the mirrors. You've got to be kidding. Those two know better than that. Okay. What? Are you serious? They don't want the other groups to come. Give me a break. They're going to label 175 kids because two screwed up. Okay. Send them in when you get back.

Principal: *Well?*

Student A: Okay, it was already in there, you know we wouldn't plan anything like this. I sprayed it on the mirror. Only one word.

Principal: *And?*

Student B: And I wrote one word on the other mirror.

Principal: *That's it. From what I heard there was shaving cream and toilet paper all over the place.*

Student B: Well, it wasn't us. And no one else went in there after us. You can ask Mr. B. Maybe some of their workers did it (Note: which, by the way, did turn out to be the case).

Principal: *Do you understand the consequences of this?*

Student A: Yep, they told us and boy is everyone going to be mad at us. Does the rest of our team and the other team know they can't go on their community service trips there?

Principal: *I am sure the word is out. Guys, I can't believe this. You're on a community service field trip. Stuffing bags, carrying toys, carrying food, helping others. And what do you do? I am really surprised in you two especially.*

Student A: I really am sorry. It was a stupid thing to do, but can I say just one other thing. I can't believe that lady yelled at us in front of everybody and told them that it was all our fault that the others couldn't come back to help.

Principal: *You know how I feel about the yelling and in front of the others, but it is because of you two that the others can't come back. I will call you back to the office at announcements to let you know what's next.*

PHONE RINGS ...

Parent: I was shocked. Your kids were working so hard and then the two boys did what they did. I can't believe it. That woman just yelled and yelled at the boys and then the whole group. And the two of them had been two of the hardest working all morning. One of them was in my group.

Principal: *Well, I appreciate the perspective. The kids did work hard. Still, the boys made a mistake and there needs to be a consequence for that. It's a shame the others have to pay for their actions, too.*

Parent: That's true, and there's a lesson in all of that, too. But I just wanted to let you know it wasn't as bad as she made it seem.

AT LUNCH ...

Teacher: Well? Did they tell you everything?

Principal: *I think so. What do you mean?*

Teacher: Well, that, uh, woman, really chewed on them in front of the other kids. Called them all kinds of names and yelled at all the kids, how they didn't want "little kids" to help out in the first place. I mean, those kids worked their tails off for three hours doing some heavy duty lifting and packaging. And, you know what, I think one of their workers added to the mess in the bathroom. These students are usually pretty honest, even when they screw up.

PHONE RINGS ...

Superintendent:

> The woman from the help center just called. She told me that the boys trashed a bathroom. I expect you're going to suspend them?

Principal: *I haven't suspended a student all year except for Peter's poor judgment at the dance. I think what I have in mind will have a much greater impact on the boys and the entire class.*

Superintendent:

> You need to teach them a lesson, and the others need to get a strong message. How will the parents know what you've done if you don't suspend them?

Later that day: Principal and the boys

"Okay, here's the deal." (What would YOU do? <u>SEE CHOICES BELOW!</u>)

CHOICE 1

Okay, here's the deal. We have to make an impression on the others. You kids just can't do stuff like this and get away with it. You're both out, five days. You can make up your work. That starts tomorrow. No winter concert tonight, no dance Friday night. You'll be back in school next Wednesday morning. I'll call your folks now to let them know. Go get your books that you think you'll need and come back here.

CHOICE 2

Okay, here's the deal. First, we're going back there right now — you can take the late bus home. Clean up time. Then, tomorrow before block starts, we're going to have a class meeting. I will tell them why the other community service trips this week are called off and I expect each of you to have something to say to your classmates, with sincerity. And I will be the judge of that. After school detention today. You both can play in the concert tonight but no dance for you Friday night. And, on the next field trip, you stay back.

CHOICE 3

Okay, here's the deal. It's real simple. You each have a handbook. This should be familiar. Vandalism. I'll call it a category B instead of A since it wasn't premeditated, but still, it's vandalism. First offense. Three day suspension and you're on warning for the remainder of the trimester. Get your books, be back here in five minutes.

YOUR CALL? 1? 2? 3?

Illusory? Constructive? Technical?

Issue: The Achievement Gap

CHOICE A

Let's be honest. We are not going to see leaps in test scores. How do we expect poor kids from single parent homes to excel? The kids are on at the bus stop at 5:45 a.m. and some don't get home from intramurals and detention until 6:00 p.m. They probably go home to an empty house. I am amazed the kids are doing as well as they are. Let's just proceed the way we have been until the kids feel more comfortable. Some have only been in the district for a year or two. The others have been remediated since the start of elementary school and it didn't work. How are we now supposed to make a big difference. We can't solve society's problems overnight. Anyway, some of the kids are succeeding. Two of them (them?) are in the chorus and my student council representative this trimester is from the city. Just wait 'til February. The whole community will see how much we're doing and so will the kids. We're doing the best we can.

CHOICE B

Let's be honest. We are not going to see leaps in test scores and may not know the effects of this effort for years. But, it's the right thing to do. There's not just one answer. It's writing across the curriculum. It's doing the labs and making observations of the data. Algebra? Yes. Ok, some concepts will be over their heads but some won't. And we'll figure out who needs more, and we'll bring the kids back for a second period of math. That's when you can bring them up in the basics. You can't accelerate learning without adding time. And, we need models. The kids need to see as many professionals as possible.

It all boils down to expectations. When s/he walks through the door, do we see a college student, a junior college student, or someone with no future at all? If you send the message that "I know you can't do this" then the student will live down to that expectation.

After–school help sessions. Parent meetings closer to home. Home visits. Teacher mentors. These are all pieces and together they may work. We just need to keep trying harder and fitting more into our intervention systems.

CHOICE C

Test scores. No problem. The new groupings in math and English will really help. The computer programs we are using in both areas are targeted to objectives on both the state norm test and the standardized test we just switched to. And the report to the standards accreditation office this year is going to show an 18% increase in time spent on math and reading. We've put three new programs in place this year after school and even the Saturday help sessions. And did you know that 40% of the students from the city have been in our district for less than two years. How are we supposed to catch those kids up overnight? When we disaggregate the data, you'll see kids who have been here since first grade doing significantly better. We're doing the best we can.

Constructive?
Technical?
Illusory?

Once again, you make the call.

on constructive schooling

This constructivism brings us into dangerous territory.

(I rarely use the term.)

Because, all we need to do is start labeling schools, instruction, curriculum, and beliefs as "constructivist," and we'll have the religious right, the anti-OBE folks, and the high school teachers all over us.

And, once we begin clarifying the term and pairing it with schools that are making a difference by anyone's standards, the technocrats, bureaucrats, and foundations would start developing "checklists to accomplish constructivism" further allowing others to be against it and turning it into a technical process. The next thing you know, we'll have the constructivist diet.

On the other hand, it has great potential for our consideration of successful schooling. You see, there's a bottom line here and it's not programs, great lesson plans, pedagogy, authentic assessment, technology applications, interdisciplinary units, integrated learning, whole language, parts language, field study, or counselors teaching.

It is not teaming, advisory, exploratory blocks, block scheduling, co-curricular activities, or school-wide interdisciplinary themes.

Constructive schooling promotes more depth and a deeper look at schooling. The bottom line? Democratic principles. Justice. Respect for persons. Equity. A hopeful future focus.

When Popkewitz and colleagues were finished, what they had assessed was a look at several schools. They sought to look at IGE implementation. They discovered schools which defined work, knowledge, and authority in different ways. The relationships among those categories were differentiated by principles that matter.

on constructive (as opposed to technical/illusory) culture and thinking about middle school

Team field trips correlating subjects are critical. Kept in perspective, they are only a means to achieving successful teaming and interdisciplinary study and all the attributes that we aspire to accomplish through their use.

Teaming and interdisciplinary study are critical. Kept in perspective, they are only a means to applying beliefs that accept the contribution of every student; expect every student can and will contribute; recognize that relevance, experience, and discovery are essential to achievement; and respect that belongingness, competence, and empowerment are necessary to foster self-esteem and achievement.

And, these practices, these programs and systems, these beliefs are all critical. Kept in perspective, they are only a means of achieving the principles of equity, opportunity, and hope.

The Geometry Unit

THE DISPLAY...

"Class, these are beautiful. I have never seen reports done as well done as these. Your lines are so crisp and clean. Mark, your string plot is extraordinary. And Martha, your poster is gorgeous. You know class, these are going to be put up in the foyer of the district office. I am really proud of your work. Johan, do you want to read your summary of the project that will get posted with the projects?"

"And Beth, show everyone your picture of Pythagoras. Didn't she do a beautiful sketch? You all worked so hard on these. Okay, let's see how you did on your homework problems."

***

(continued)

THE DISPUTE ...

"Brent, number 5. Ted, 6. Alice, 7. Annie, 8. Write big and be sure to number the steps in your proof."

"I didn't get number 6. I tried it one way and got one answer and then when I checked it I thought I should have used a different theorem. Are there two ways to solve that?"

"Ted, sit down then. Okay, Allen, you put number 6 up. Ted, I don't know where you got confused. The answer key shows clearly which steps to take. Allen will have it up in a minute, I am sure."

"Well, I even drew it out, like one of those string plots to show the two ways I solved it."

"Ted, we are not in art class and I don't do posters in math. Do you see anything about drawings in the directions on page 107? Class, do any of you see anything about drawings on page 107? I didn't think so. Ted, sit."

THE DISCUSSION ...

"We don't get it!"

"Come on boys – you've been over here playing around for ten minutes. Perhaps a lesson in time management is needed for homeroom next week."

"Yeah, we know, 'Avoiding Distractions 101.'"

"So, what's the problem?"

"We just don't get it. We all understand down to this step. Then we're stuck. Marvin thinks we should apply that theorem that says all the angles have to equal 180 degrees here. I say it's just a simple axiom, if a=b, b=a. That applies to angles, too, doesn't it? That's why it's 90 degrees."

"Well, what does that tell you?"

"We're both right. There are two ways to solve this one."

"Right. What's that expression? 'There are several roads to Rome'"

"No, that's Romey's: 'Eat in, Take out, or Drive Through. It's still a Romey's Burger."

"Please. Okay, I want you to wrap up these next eight problems. Then go back and find at least three of the proofs that could be solved more than one way and be ready to present them to the class tomorrow. You can kick it off with your burger commercial. You've got fifteen minutes. Use it. Hey, and I want a string plot using the geo boards to illustrate at least one of the problems unless you have some other way to show your result. A poster or something will do fine. You could do burgers and angles: a geometric collage with steak sauce."

One more time:
You make the call.

more on constructive culture

Stop and take a look. Next time you are at a fast food restaurant, the post office (now there's a group that is unfairly maligned – at least in our town we're talking next day delivery anywhere and quite friendly with that efficiency I might add), the license bureau (we're talking about a group of not very happy "take a number" "no renewals on Tuesdays" "no social security card, no license" campers), an amusement park, or any organization that has a variety of employees and a language of its own, just sit back, watch, and listen.

Who's in charge? How do you know? Where does their authority come from? The uniform? The title? Where do they sit, stand, or work? How are they addressed? Are they respected?

Who's really in charge? How did you figure that out? Is it the same person?

What are the goals of the employees? What's important to them? Are they there to serve first, take care of themselves second? Are they more interested in serving you or in when their next break takes place?

How is success defined? Numbers of burgers served? Employees of the month? Happy customers? Making it through the day?

Constructive? Technical? Illusory?

Try It . It Works.

Then, go back to school and sit, watch, listen, and ...

One more thought on constructive culture analysis

If you go around labeling and categorizing every action and decision, all you've become is the culture police applying a technical analysis to what should be a constructive process.

This constructivist thing is a way to look at the world. It is a lens taken out of a drawer full of gadgets. It is different ways to see the world.

When the language of constructivism, technical, or illusory perspectives is useful, use it. When the language of Dewey and the progressives is appropriate, use it. When the characteristics and assumptions of Vars, Lounsbury, and the middle school forefathers are applicable, apply them.

The Constructive Middle School

E mbedded in the history of middle level education are the language and artifacts of *reform, restructuring,* and *paradigm shifts.*

Middle level mission statements are characterized by *beliefs* about democracy, society, and children as well as prescriptions, programs, and policies for schooling. Vars' original assumptions and beliefs which promote concepts of democracy, justice, equity, self-worth, values, and success through experience have prevailed.

Educational *concepts* of collaboration, non-competitiveness, school membership, and others permeate and school vision statements and planning documents.

Programs and practices of teaming, advisories, and intramural sports continue to be implemented based on these principles rather than traditional practices.

Successful middle schools, those celebrated for their "blue ribbon" status and those quietly saving children, illustrate threads of beliefs, concepts, and practices intertwined in their success. This tapestry woven from convictions and daily effort is middle school.

Summary — Applying Attributes to Culture and Applying Attributes of Culture To Successful Schooling

One can explore the culture of the middle school in terms of political structures. Looking at the school on the organizational chart, one can examine the culture in terms of knowledge, work, and authority in relation to one another and in terms of their definition and impact in the network of the elements. Beyond the individual "bits" or the framework of components, the political perspective of the culture explores relationships, the cause-effect relationships, the collaboration, and essentially the "schema" of the organization.

One can explore the culture in terms of knowledge, work, and authority and in terms of other principles which underlie the culture. Where do principles of equity and opportunity fit into the discussion of the input? Does the philosophy truly drive the practice and serve as a filter for the input? When one utters "at this school we do 'it' this way," do they mean the isolated practice, the practice in terms of its frame with others, the practice and its interrelated impact on the knowledge, work, authority, and self of the organization, or the practice and its perspective of democratic principles, emphasis on self-concept, its impact on justice and respect for others, and so on?

Using types of culture in describing the school as technical, illusory, and constructive, describing "it" in a school could necessitate a "micro" analysis of a particular practice or program. The cultural aspect evolves, however, from the individual's framing of the item and talking about it rather than within the item itself. Depending on how a particular item is framed by the catalyst determines how effective the item is by itself, how it determines the culture, and consequently, how it fits in to a scheme of cultural determinism which essentially affects personnel and future decisions.

An example will clarify and simplify the above. An advisory might be perceived as "illusory" if a school states "we've got one" and goes through the motions. It could be categorized "technical" if the school "counts" the successful lessons, minutes per week of instruction, and students involved, without having an internalized investment in it. And it could be categorized "constructive" if it fits into a bigger picture, is framed for reasons cited in terms of beliefs about students and the school's mission, and fosters the evolution of the program rather than establishing a packaged, fixed program in isolation.

Last, the culture of the school and the school itself is the sum of its parts. If all the pieces are embedded with success, there, logically, is a better chance that the school will be successful. Again, the "micro" analysis might reveal constructive practices throughout the school as numerous sub-units and, therefore, sub-cultures exist in a school. As principles of synergy apply, the impact of the total has greater strength than simply the sum of the strength of the parts. Numerous constructive sub-cultures and practices do not insure a constructive school. At the "macro" level, the culture is the intertwining of sub-units framed not by organizational charts or ceremonies of the corporate culture but rather the cognitive framing of the sub-units and the subsequent cognitive action practiced by the principal.

***

> So, it's time to slow down. It's time to hold up a mirror. Where are YOU in all of this? Where is your school? Where are your programs and practices? Your beliefs? Your tests? Your conversations? My suggestion: go back and read these parts again - slowly - with feeling - and think for a while.

Summary

Culture is ...

(or an exercise in redundancy, not to mention that this page gets pretty deep)

a concept in itself but essentially, a network of intertwined concepts with overlapping attributes and exemplars. Again, it is more than the packaged programs, innovations, research based instruction, technical practices, or essentials of curriculum. It is more, too, than the combination of these items in a "network" of the school, organization of the components, or even causal relationship among school factors.

Individually, a program or practice, as an entity in itself, can be "successful." Similarly, when the causal relationships and interactions among sub-units are developed, they, too, can "be successful." There must be a commonality among the parts, among the relationships, and beyond the network. The success must be found in the underlying principles.

The constructive middle school culture includes attributes and exemplars of:

- concepts of collaboration,

- integration of useful knowledge,

- experiential learning and application of skills and knowledge,

- empowered learners and faculty,

- meaningful work and relevance,

- self-esteem building,

- exemplars of democracy,

- a curriculum which fosters a future focused role image,

- modeling and practices of citizenship,

- intentional efforts at relationship building,

and more.

Whether the practice is a month long field experience, cooperative learning strategies, or a traditional vocabulary lesson, the essential ingredient to citing "success" in the school is the explained rationale for these items, the meaning that underpins them, the contexts in which they are placed, the process by which they came to exist, and their "relationship" to the whole. "Success" is founded in all of these factors, applying all and more of the principles cited above to each, in a synergistic network of all selected and rejected items.

CHAPTER 7 Applying the Logic: Principles, Patterns, and Practices

We've established some common sense aspects of successful middle schools and hammered away at culture. But developing successful middle schools must go beyond a plethora (how many in a plethora?) of good ideas and controversial stances in isolation. It's even more than culture (I know, I said everything is culture). There must be some connection between what we spout off about and what we do. There must be some means of achieving that culture by design rather than accident.

We hear often "that's against middle school philosophy." What exactly does that mean? An examination of the practice usually means it's not age appropriate. But the need goes well beyond that simple litmus test.

What we need to understand and scrutinize and test and clarify and struggle with and think about is why we do what we do. *Why do we do what we do?* Do we do teaming for the sake of doing teaming? Do we have advisory because most middle schools do? Why bother with all the work of interdisciplinary units?

It comes down to connections and consistency. It comes down to knowing our purpose. It comes down to establishing patterns of work that connect our principles and our practices.

That is where one finds success in middle schooling (and all schooling).

(THIS PART IS GOOD – READ IT CAREFULLY)
Why is middle school successful?
Simple.
Middle school STARTS with the kids – who they are developmentally, intellectually, etc. – and with what we want them to KNOW and be able to DO ...
THEN middle school considers the conversations, the systems, the models, the frameworks, and concepts that help organize how we achieve that end ... and
THEN middle school develops the structures and ideas and practices and innovations and programs that FIT INTO those systems which allow us to achieve those ends.
Middle school systems and frameworks link our practices, old and new, with our beliefs and principles.
It's sort of like democracy. It starts with a preamble, a set of guiding principles and beliefs (which are reinforced by the Bill of Rights). It follows with a system of government, checks and balances, separation of powers, a legislative process and so on. Then, and only then, do we get bogged down with the daily practices and routines which are supposed to fit into the systems and be consistent with the principles.

on why this is so important

What is truly at risk, and the concept that reinforces the status of restructuring (which is synonymous with successful schooling and middle school), (still with me?) are concepts of democracy, playing on the same level playing field, and hope. (Are you still with me? Are you catching those clues on successful schooling?)

It appears that in every era when America (and educational reform) begins to toy with legitimate equity and equality, a cluster of elite my-kid-must-go-to-Harvard parents pair up with aspiring politician pseudo-educators (you know the kind, the educational leaders who talk about their two years of teaching and their one year as a principal as a "wealth of experience") to ensure that separate and unequal remain the status quo.

Hence, we will move into the twenty-first century stuck with Carnegie units, six period days, and tracking in high schools; fighting battles of reading groups, remedial math, phonics, and pull out programs in elementary schools; and constant tampering and pleas for "academic rigor" in the middle schools ... all settled in traditional school periods scheduled into traditional school days packed into traditional school years.

(Did you catch the conflict there? The lack of connections? Democracy and equity in one paragraph and practices and programs in the other. Guess what's missing? Systems! Frameworks! Models!)

It all has to fit all the time, without thinking about it!

Means and ends.

If-then.

So what?

Why?

Why not?

Purpose.

Priorities.

Scenario: The Interview

Principal: *Mr. M., thank you for coming in for the interview today. I know you have been interviewing most of the morning with faculty, so I have just a few questions. Could you describe a middle school student? Let's get past the point that they are different. Give me some similarities.*

Teacher: Middle school kids need activity, they are curious, they love to socialize.

Principal: *So what? In other words, how does that affect you?*

Teacher: It should affect every planning decision I make. They need to do lab work, hands-on activities, interdisciplinary units, field study, two to three different activities a class period, get to the library, select topics on their own. And, it means I need to be a good listener and pick up on cues of student interests and motivators.

Principal: *Let's say I suggest that we are going to adopt the new Concerned Discipline Program. Three teachers went off to a conference and said it's just what we need. How would you react?*

Teacher: After hearing more about it, my initial reaction would be, is it a match? Does it fit with what I and, hopefully, the school believes about how to treat kids? Is it within my belief system, the school's, yours, and the community? Is it consistent with how I run my science lab, how we operate on field trips, the characteristics of responsible kids that we hope to foster? Is it a fit with our school philosophy? I guess I would ask questions like that; oh, and is it flexible? or am I stuck with a locked-in program?

As has been hinted — or has been harped on — throughout this text, is the value of systems to link principles and practices. Small-is-better is the principle which guides us to teaming which is how we fit in double periods and team assemblies. When we go off to a middle school conference and steal a great idea, do we attempt to fit it into an existing system of curriculum, an existing unit, or a structure? Do we throw out what we are doing and replace it with the new idea? (Remember the baby, the bath water, and the tub?) Or do we add it on to the list of other programs and practices which occur unconnected. It needs to fit. And there should be a good reason to include it.

PRINCIPLES

PATTERNS

PRACTICES

Change and Middle Schooling

An *innovation* is traditionally a singular program with a distinct set of attributes, exemplified by only itself (presumably there are no perceived "other ways to do it").

Change viewed as *reform* is generally the implementation of a particular program or series of events which are interrelated as part of a broader plan. This plan, representative of more abstract concepts, is characterized by a set of attributes common to each of the elements of the reform and by a determining tendency or rationale which justifies the plan.

Change cited as *principle-based or utopian* parallels the use of assumptions or universals to guide practice. These are generally abstract and complex concepts representative of guiding principles. This is where change is focused on the ends, the core beliefs of the organization and its mission rather than "having one of those." The specific product of change is not nearly as significant as the outcomes for which it is an exemplar.

Understandings from language and communication may help here. Apply the scheme of simple concept, abstract concept, and universal concept to those responsible for reviewing good ideas; for change must consider where things fit – how they fit in.

For example, consider the following. Do we plan the guidance component for our school beginning with a specific packaged guidance program in mind, the goal to implement an advisory program in the school, or the mission to establish meaningful and significant relationships between students and adults in the school? Each might result in the exact same product, an advisor/advisee program with specific operational characteristics. The differencs is in the process of implementation. Start with the principles, then establish the system, then select the program to fit in. Means and ends. Purpose. Understanding the "why?"

Concepts.

Maybe this will help, especially for the left-brainers who like the use of categories, definitions, and lists.

Recalling the previous discussion about concepts (if everything is culture then concepts are everything), a concept can be so finite that there is no other example of it except for itself; it can be general enough to have several examples but all with the same attributes; or, it can be a universal characterized by its unique intangible attributes and its "essence." (sorry.)

Huh?

Think about it this way.

Simple concept:
this chair in my room is the only one of its kind.

Abstract concept:
Chairs – legs, a seat, a place to sit

Universal concept:
Chairness – I can sit on it – or it represents something that something or someone can rest upon.

(got the idea of applying language theory to what's around us?)

Simple concept:
Innovation

Abstract concept:
Reform

Universal concept:
Principle-based change.

Simple concept:
A four-person team, four periods a day

Abstract concept:
Teaming

Universal concept:
A sense of connectedness; making a big school seem small; community.

Here's a little test.

Most middle schools have teams. Most put mathematics, science, English, and social studies teachers on the team with some variations for language, geography, reading, or some other "core" area.

Why?

Why is math on the team? It's the toughest subject to integrate and their grouping of students throws off all the other classes. Why not art? Why not a humanities team? Why not a technology and quantitative reasoning team?

Is teaming - a "core team" - the end, or a means?

The principles, the beliefs that should drive teaming, are those of connecting kids and teachers, making the big school smaller, seeking logical interdisciplinary connections, communications efficiency, and others. THOSE are what matters. Pairing the English teacher with the social studies teacher is a means to that end. But how often do we make subsequent decisions to fit the connection between English and social studies instead of fitting our beliefs about kids and connections?

Doesn't it make more sense to study the history of the Renaissance when the art teacher is teaching Van Gogh and the science teacher Galileo? On the other hand, why don't we teach economics in math, balancing equations, and symmetry when studying democracy, checks and balances, government? Or why not study eco-systems and industrial technology systems when studying government and how a bill becomes a law?

Why?

Why not?

Perhaps understanding the concept of concepts helps you think about it a little differently.

on change – as you think about middle school

History reflects the great waves of change through the agricultural foundations, the industrial revolution, the computer age, and now an information era. Communities, politics, economics, and education all have their roots and realities embedded in these periods of history. Whereas business, medicine, and other professions have led the way or reacted to these periods of American history, education still finds itself driven by the agricultural calendar and the industrial model of efficient-educate the masses-assembly line-early twentieth century mentality of schooling.

Some individual schools have attempted to break the traditional organizational molds. Only middle school as an entity, however, conceptually and in practice, has situated itself in the late twentieth century and prepared itself for the twenty-first. The middle school movement has become convincing enough to outlive the fad delineation and perhaps even the "self esteem building whole child" mind set of its adversaries. Whether it survives the wave of elitism and conservatism remains to be seen.

As goes the middle school; so goes reform.

Middle school may not fall in the same category as the cotton gin, conveyor belts, Sputnik, and computers as catalysts for societal change. Middle school, however, symbolizes a paradigm shift, one exemplified by reflective professional practice, "cognitive/cultural" leadership, and authentic education.

Remember? Middle school builds schools around kids, literally and figuratively.

Time will tell if that is enough. Too many folks think that schooling and the latest issue of reform comprise a political playing field for the conservatives and liberals to fight it out on. They forget that reform should be about the kids and the future. But, just to make sure we have a job when the anti-reformers and politicians who don't know education are finished, I wouldn't throw out that McGuffey reader, the rusty dissection knife, or your slide rule just yet.

Principles, Patterns, and Practices

Consider "standard" or now "traditional" middle school *practices:* teaming, core blocks, advisory programs, exploratory wheels, and others. Are they valuable in all middle schools? Are they the criteria for the successful middle school? Do they fit within systems of the school? Do they achieve the mission and principles upon which the school is driven? Or, do they reside in isolation and are cited for their intrinsic value when and where appropriate?

Consider standard middle school *patterns, systems, and concepts:* heterogeneous grouping, mainstreaming, research, inquiry and exploration, self-esteem building, organizational structures, focus on organizational skills. Are the practices of the school congruent with these concepts? Are there policies, systems, or models to insure these concepts as rationale for practices or do the practices and programs sit in isolation? Do the practices of the school connect within this broader scheme.

Think about standard or traditional middle school *principles and beliefs:* equity, democratic principles, beliefs that every child can learn, celebrating diversity, professional growth. Are these embedded in every practice and system? Are they reflected in meaningless slogans and banners or are they "institutionalized" within the systems of the school? Are they considered in all decision making by councils and teams of adults (and students), reflective of the democratic principles they espouse?

This is the last page of this chapter (wow, pretty short chapter)

Well, yes. But the point is as simple as it is sophisticated. Discussing principles, patterns of practice or systems, and practices sounds rather lofty and certainly of low priority for the middle school practitioner. On the other hand, it's a pretty simple concept: consistency between theory and practice, between what we believe and what we do, is found in systems and frameworks. When they are in place, new ideas can be "fit in" (or not) and the reasons will prevail. When they are absent, we lose the original reasons for what we do and begin to do things because we've always done it that way, or worse, we begin to give up what matters. See how it plays out.

Try it out.

Pick a middle school "thing" (It's really too bad our teachers taught us not to use words like "thing" or "stuff" in writing when often they say it all.)

Teaming.
The block schedule.
Intramurals.
A particular lesson that clicked with the kids.

1. What principles drive that particular "thing"?

2. Are they consistent with the principles that drive the school?

3. Does it fit into an existing system? Or, is it a system itself?

4. What are some of the practices or procedures used to "deliver" it?

5. Do they fit in well?

In other words, does the "thing" fit in? Are the principles, systems, and practices consistent and connected? If so, it's a fit. Try it with one of your school's systems or practices. And, in addition to the questions above, ask if those responsible for implementing this and those who benefit from it know the rationale and answers to these five questions.

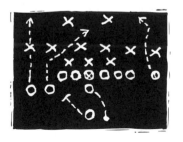

Applying the Logic: Principles, Patterns, and Practices ■

CHAPTER 8 Thinking About Middle School

The most poetical experiences of my life have been those moments of conceptual comprehension of a few of the extraordinary generalized principles and their complex interactions that are apparently employed in the governance of universal evolution.

– R. Buckminster Fuller

(R E A D   S L O W L Y)

Middle schools are cultures. Everything is culture. Middle school, as does reform, with a set of beliefs and systems (not a dusty philosophy and a collection of programs), has a constructivist culture embedded in its development. Constructivism, like its corollary technical/illusory cultures, defines how we work, our relationships, authority, and knowledge as revealed by what we do, say, think, and act. Constructivism, by its very nature, is embedded with success ranging from happy kids going home complaining about too much research to teachers causing every child to think and do.

When we implement schools/classes/(even programs), we either maintain their constructivist nature and potential by holding firm to our/its beliefs and not tampering with systems, or we worry too much about the pressures of the world and test scores and politics and end up with a technical or illusory culture. We either model and base our decisions and teachable moments on issues like respect, social justice, meaningful achievement, useful knowledge, and responsibility ... or we don't.

Do we want democracy or not? That's the bottom line.

The Principal as Leader of Change

The "successful" middle school is a middle school with a "constructive" culture. That point has been established. The concept of the successful middle school is denoted by significant attributes and exemplified by schools where all of the elements work in connection, collaboration, and in "synergy" with others.

Analysis illustrates that the successful middle school, the culture of the middle school, can be affected by several components categorized as the school entity itself, from sub-units within, or by external policy and forces. Concurrently, all "input" must be reviewed and either incorporated, negotiated, or rejected in the operation, organization, and essentially, the culture of the school. These components are realized through the policy statements of the school, the personnel in the school, the delivery of the "messages" by the personnel, or the practices of the school.

Whereas particular elements of the school are affected by policy, faculty, staff, administrators, parents, and students can selectively comply or choose not to comply with policy depending on the emphasis placed on each item. Whether the policy reflects a judicial mandate for desegregation or a stipulation to implement the results of curriculum review, the interpretation and subsequent implementation by administrators and teachers vary significantly from site to site.

School personnel logically are critical in the interpretation and implementation of opinions and criticism. Depending on the position, accessibility, and role of the individual, the impact of the issues for review can be quite strong or moot. It is at this stage that one questions the administrator of the successful school with "how did you get here?" and "where is it all going?" rather than the traditional question posed in effective schools of "what have you got?"

That point is important - it is the blend of reading the culture and planning. "What have you got?" doesn't matter. What matters is "how'd you get here? Why do you do it this way? Where's it going?"

In many cases, the individual as catalyst is only moderately successful in implementing or choosing not to implement change depending upon how the messages are delivered and the receptivity and nurturing of the recipients. On the other hand, leaders with outstanding "leadership style"

and ability to motivate through communication may not have the vision or perspective on the successful culture to "make it happen."

In many schools designated as "effective" the sole question posed is "what have you got?" In these illusory schools it appears that change emanates directly from changes in practice. And, in addition decisions are usually designed to insure the decision-makers are "being right" rather than "doing right." Giving the illusion of success, the change is usually superficial and lasts as long as the packaged product is in vogue and is supported by the isolated individual who implemented the change.

So, if middle school is "embedded" as a constructivist venture, why are so many technical and illusory ventures?

One person sorts input from state and district forces, balancing the initiatives of the individuals and sub-groups in the school, and monitoring the school's progress as an entity itself. That one person is the principal.

The principal is the ~~catalyst~~ spark - conductor - architect - gardener - teacher - who causes change to occur or not to occur.

(Catalyst is struck out on purpose. It's a great word to use when discussing change, but catalysts don't change when the chemical reaction begins. Leaders must grow - or no one does.)

In the technical school, it is the principal who simply imposes standards, checklists, forms, and formulae for success or reduces the success embedded stuff to that level.

In the illusory school, it is the principal who adopts new innovative programs from publishers or other schools in order to "have one of those, too" or to "match up" with the latest reform report or effective schools check list and reduces the success embedded stuff to that level.

In the constructivist school, it is the principal, who scrutinizes all input through his or her lens, thinks about it within his or her cognitive framework, and leads, causing "it" to happen!

Period.

The Test

PART 1

> *My kid has had the best years ever in elementary school. She attended a private school for a few years and the public school that feeds your school for the past three years. Her teachers have really got her focused, on task, and accomplishing so much. I hope YOU can continue that in middle school.*

We've all heard comments like this.

How do we react? Do we "hand schedule" the student? Do we have to put her off team to be with the "right" teachers? Are we confident that the entire faculty reads and attends I.E.P.s and does not abdicate their responsibility to the resource room when reading time comes along? Are we confident that the teacher will contact the parents before the year begins to find out what the areas of success and interest were in elementary school? Will they contact the elementary teacher to find out what worked? Will they monitor her progress early on because if she gets behind it will be a lost year? Are we confident that the curriculum is flexible enough to challenge the student?

Play it out. With that one little comment from a parent, where is your level of confidence? How well do you know the systems in your school? your classroom? your district? Are those systems embedded with principles that you would go to the line for? Are the ends and means clearly distinguished? Are they connected?

Teachers make hundreds of decisions a day in planning and on their feet. Principals receive input which moves their decision making from the reactionary to the proactive (sorry, I hate that word, too) to the major planning efforts. The question of all questions is: how do you deal with the input?

PART 2 - "in-basket" exercises

If you really want to know where YOU stand and want to read YOUR culture - spend a little time on these. Play out the scenarios. What you do they say to you? How do you react? Who is involved? Does the reaction reflect what you believe about those thirteen year olds? Is it consistent "with middle school philosophy?" with what we know about kids? with what parents expect? Is it *technical? illusory? constructive?*

How do you read/react to ...

"I just came back from this convention and saw the neatest program."

"I just finished signing the progress reports for the entire seventh grade. Very thorough. Do you realize how many of you commented on homework not being turned in?"

"Mr. Vanderbilt just yelled at his class, again."

"The I.E.P. team recommends that we classify Robert as learning disabled."

"We're stuck. Half of us want to purchase a text and the other half wants to continue writing our own units."

"We're tired of the arts teachers feeling like second-class citizens around here."

"We want to take a group on an ocean expedition."

"I'd like to do a musical this year. Cast of thousands. Anyone who tries out and is willing to show up for rehearsal is in."

"We're walking over to the zoo at 10:30."

"Line three. It's the superintendent."

"I can't find my retainer. It was on my tray."

"We want every eighth grader in Algebra. Only two levels — high and higher."

"My conferences were great tonight. All but one kid's parents made it."

"Quick, Danny has a gun! He just shot two kids, help!"

PART 3
In the situations above ...

What percentage of your administrators would be able to predict *your* response/reaction? _____%

The reaction of your student support personnel (counselors and others)? _____%

The reaction of your faculty?_____% central office administration? _____% Parents? _____% STUDENTS? _____%

Why do you think it is the percentage you stated?

What does this tell you about how your school responds to situations?

What does this tell you about the value of being consistent and predictable?

Does this tell you anything about the culture of your school?

RESULTS

In some cases, even most cases, hopefully, you have time to think about decisions and situations that arise. In others, you react. In all cases, you hope and trust that ...

1) you have the practices and systems in place to deal with all that needs to be dealt with;
2) people who implement those systems are on the same wavelength with you and each other;
3) built into those systems and incorporated into those reactions or in the planning, are principles of justice, fairness, respect for persons, and other democratic concepts along with those beliefs about students and professionals as well as routines for safety and security.
4) you have established a culture that makes the responses predictable to others and that they are consistent in philosophy and practice.

Whether the situation is a quick response or the product of well thought out planning, it's *still* "all culture."

And if you approach the world that way, then comes the knowledge that each teacher, team, area, office, department, and whatever groups exist know their part in the bigger system. You have the confidence that each has systems and priorities in place. And *that* is why culture is so critical. That is why and how we do things around here – not the legislated procedures, not the prescriptions, but what you see/hear/observe/decide/sense – is essential.

Whether it's all the systems that must kick into place when a student has a gun, how you react to a lost retainer, or your contribution to the math curriculum committee, folks expect and count on consistency and the ability to say, "that's how we do it in middle school; that's how we do it here." And, hopefully, no one has tampered with those systems to the extent that they no longer serve as adequate means to the principled–ends that drove them initially.

And, that "that's how" is related to what we know and think and feel and expect of early adolescents and to what we know and think and feel and expect of the growth of adults as well as kids and to what we know and think and feel and expect of useful knowledge, meaningful work, and professional relationships among kids and adults.

Another Test:

An Exercise in Symmetry, Planning Chaos, or Reading the Culture and Planning the Successful School

There is not much difference in reading the culture of your classroom or school and planning your classroom or school. The former entails looking at everything around you through your lens and making sense of it. The latter entails taking everything in your brain and projecting it outward through your lens. (This could get complicated if we get into shared vision, but that, too, is another book.) Both reading the culture or planning one (if that's possible) are necessary functions of successful middle schooling since nothing in middle school is ever set in stone and we're always planning ahead.

So, what do we know about the process of successful middle schooling?

Reading the culture or designing your classroom/school for successful schooling requires:

—discovering what one believes, how one organizes what s/he does, and how one acts. When all three are blended in the design - when all three are considered in the blueprints - success is built in. Consequently, one must look at the artifacts of the organization to discover what principles and beliefs guide the school, how people and things are organized, and how people and things work on a daily basis.

—reading the blueprints (architectural, handbooks, procedural manuals, signs on the walls, and the unwritten rules). What is embedded in the planning and propositions for the organization?

—knowing individuals and understanding the relationships desired and existing among them.

—determining how and what adults (as well as students, the community, and others) are expected to grow and learn, respectively, and whether they are expected to "think about" the organization.

The reader with a trained eye, ear, and sixth sense for success will see the integration of beliefs, systems, and practices in the organization. S/he will recognize the consistency among them in the planning documents, the vision statements, the action plans, the annual goals, and the daily work of the school.

The other day I bumped into an architect friend at a dinner. He told me about a middle school he was proposing for a neighboring district. Within minutes he was sketching on his napkin an outline of the school. What most would see was a sketch of a building? What I saw were his beliefs about kids, what's worth knowing, and successful schooling all revealed in one two-minute sketch. He had taken the principles and systems of successful schooling and put them into a drawing so effectively that those principles were apparent in the design.

So, now it's your turn. Well, it's been your turn throughout the text if you have a pen in your hand and have marked up the margins. But just in case you haven't or if you like the structure of a workbook/textbook, now you really do have to get to work.

For the pages that follow, you may consider the way it is at your school or you may envision your ideal middle school - or better yet, go through this twice and compare the two!

Draw a page of middle school kids. (Oh go ahead, no one's looking.) Or, draw a composite of the middle school kid. Better yet, list everything you know and believe about sixth graders - seventh graders - eighth graders.

(Well, did you do it? If not, remember your reaction and response to the "assignment" the next time you ask a thirteen year old to sing or draw or write or run - alone.)

Now, list twenty things middle school youngsters must know and learn and be able to do.

(Do you think this is how Fulghum came up with his kindergarten list?)

Ever try visualization? It's the process of closing your eyes and watching yourself go through some event quite successfully, anticipating the adventures and prospects that abound. Runners visualize themselves at the starting line, feeling the crowd at the start, running up a hill, grabbing a cup of water, dashing the last quarter mile across the finish line hearing the roaring crowd. Speakers anticipate walking across the stage to the podium, looking at three points across the hall, saying their first line.

Visualize your middle school. Park your car. Walk to the front door. Enter the building. Who do you see? What's the reception? Where do you go next? What are the kids doing? What are your colleagues doing?

Go ahead - jot down what you observe and feel.

A Work Snapshot!

Now take a snapshot of 10:00 a.m. What is every individual doing at 10:00 a.m.? Use verbs for every classroom, every office, every hallway.

Finally, take a minute and sketch YOUR middle school (real or ideal). Ask the most important question: "why?" Ask it often. "'They' put science clustered on the bottom floor. I wonder why?" "So, I put the library in the middle. Why?" "The art room is on the corner with windows everywhere. Why?" "Core classrooms are clustered but with no subject distinction. Why?" etc.

"Thoughts About Successful Middle Schooling"

by

_____

(your name goes here)

Go back to page 7.

You thought I was kidding, didn't you?

If you did write, compare the two - especially if you have really "thought about" middle school.

And, finally

It's all about successful schooling for all kids.

> Schools, especially middle schools,
> should be built around the kids,
> literally and figuratively.

Teachers make the difference.

> Principals and faculty leadership make successful schooling happen.

> Principles and beliefs should drive all that we do.

Common sense should drive all that we do, too.

> Everything
> we do
> should "fit"
> and be connected.

It's all culture.

All of the above are contingent upon how and
how often we think about middle school,
individually and collectively.

So, Getting Started

1) Think (often) about ...
   PRINCIPLES AND BELIEFS
   SYSTEMS
   PRACTICES AND ROUTINES.
2) Don't confuse principles with systems and systems with practices - and don't isolate them.
3) Distinguish between means and ends.
4) Understand cultures.
5) Understand change.
6) Recognize that every system is a culture unto itself as well as part of the culture of the school.
7) Ask "WHY?" a lot. Also ask, "why not?"
8) Make sure the adults are learning and growing.
9) Continue to act, react, and use common sense, but every once in a while, step back and think about ...

the development of kids, the growth of professionals, culture, leadership, and, of course, middle school.

P. S. I'm serious about this

I expect your comments, if you have survived, would go something like this:

So this has all been very entertaining. It made me think a little bit about some of the things we do in our school. You stirred it up a little bit and even made me re-think a few things. But all this theory about principles and systems and constructivism, please. I work with these kids seven hours a day. I (pick at least one) spend three hours a night grading papers (or) spend three nights a week at school (or) attend graduate school two nights a week. I've got colleagues coming at me from ten directions about new ideas and, yes, discipline. I've got parents telling me their kid's not being challenged. I supervise three lunch shifts, two bus loadings, and the halls all day. And the committees and central office meetings are enough to drive me crazy. And YOU'RE telling me to think about principles and systems and clarifying means and ends.

Well, YES.

Oh, the irony of it all is that the most important thing you may do tomorrow is dig into the trash can for the missing retainer.

Seriously.

References

Bates, R. J. (1987). Corporate culture, schooling, and educational administration. *Educational Administration Quarterly, 23* (4), 79-115.

Elmore, R. (1979). Reform and the culture of authority in schools. *Educational Administration Quarterly, 23* (4), 60-78.

Fuller, R. B., with Agel, J., & Fiore, Q. (1970). *I seem to be a verb.* New York: Bantam Books.

Popekewitz, T., Tabachnik, B. R., & Wehlage, G. (1982). *The myth of educational reform: A study of school responses to a program of change.* Madison, WI: The University of Wisconsin Press.

Sergiovani, T. (1987). *The Principalship.* Newton, MA: Allyn and Bacon.